Columbia University

Contributions to Education

Teachers College Series

No. 843

AMS PRESS
NEW YORK

An Experiment
in the Development of
Critical Thinking

By EDWARD M. GLASER, Ph.D.

TEACHERS COLLEGE, COLUMBIA UNIVERSITY
CONTRIBUTIONS TO EDUCATION, NO. 843

Published with the Approval of
Professor Goodwin Watson, Sponsor

BUREAU OF PUBLICATIONS
Teachers College · Columbia University
NEW YORK · 1941

Library of Congress Cataloging in Publication Data

Glaser, Edward Maynard, 1911-
   An experiment in the development of critical thinking.

   Reprint of the 1941 ed., issued in series: Teachers
College, Columbia University. Contributions to
education, no. 843.
   Originally presented as the author's thesis, Columbia.
   Bibliography: p.
   1. Thought and thinking. 2. Reasoning (Psychology)
3. Difference (Psychology) I. Title. II. Series:
Columbia University. Teachers College. Contributions
to education, no. 843.
BF441.G55 1972   153.4'2'07   79-176806
ISBN 0-404-55843-7

Reprinted by Special Arrangement with Teachers
College Press, New York, New York

From the edition of 1941, New York
First AMS edition published in 1972
Manufactured in the United States

AMS PRESS, INC.
NEW YORK, N. Y.   10003

ACKNOWLEDGMENTS

INDIRECTLY and unwittingly the intellectual godfather of this study is my first professor of logic, Professor Morris Raphael Cohen, expounder of philosophy and inspirer of a rational and humane spirit.

Among the many persons who helped me to carry through the study special thanks are due:

The five teachers of the experimental classes, Mr. Jules Bernstein, and Mrs. Marie Reilly Bernstein, of the Weequahic High School, Newark, N. J., and Mr. Louis Chutroo, Dr. George Lawton, and Mr. Sidney Mandell, of the Evander Childs High School in New York City, for their masterful teaching, splendid cooperation, and constructive criticism and suggestions for improving the lesson-unit material;

Professor Clyde R. Miller, and Miss Violet Edwards, formerly of the Institute for Propaganda Analysis, for arranging to have the Institute print the first edition of some of the Watson-Glaser Tests of Critical Thinking and for making available the educational materials and the materials on propaganda analysis in the Institute's files;

Miss Sylvia Ryack, for her consistent good spirits as well as her secretarial competence in typing and editing the manuscript and performing a considerable portion of the computational work involved in the statistical treatment of the data;

Mrs. Murray Goldberg, who ably assisted in phases of the library research, testing, and interviewing;

Professors Irving Lorge and Helen M. Walker for their counsel on statistical method at various stages of progress;

Professor Henry Simon of the English Department, who went over sections of my dissertation in careful detail and taught me a good deal about the art of writing clearly and understandably;

My brother, J. A. Glaser, whose critical suggestions in

connection with the tests and lesson units were very valuable in revising them;

Professor Goodwin Watson, my sponsor, who helped to crystallize the problem and gave illuminating counsel and guidance for many phases of the research;

The various publishers—too numerous to mention—who kindly gave permission to quote; and

Dr. Margaret E. Martin and Mrs. Ruth White Beebe, two of my friends and fellow students in the Advanced School of Education at Teachers College, for their persistent interest and encouragement, their searching, constructive criticisms, and their many helpful editorial suggestions as they read the manuscript through its several revisions.

E. M. G.

CONTENTS

Contents

Surely it is good for a great democracy that its citizens shall constantly ask their governors to give a rational account of their stewardship, that men and women shall demand that new proposals as well as the established institutions should defend themselves before the bar of reason.

—MORRIS RAPHAEL COHEN

Since democracy rests on individual rights, its chief support must come from each citizen—and its decay is from the same source. Its oldest and greatest enemy is the greed, indifference, selfishness of its members and the inequities which exist within its borders.

—THE EDUCATIONAL POLICIES COMMISSION
OF THE NATIONAL EDUCATION ASSOCIATION

In a world of barbarism peoples who no longer are willing to defend themselves and their convictions are doomed.

—EDGAR ANSEL MOWRER

CHAPTER I

Introduction

A NUMBER of the men who laid the foundations of the American political structure were keenly aware of the vital relation of education both to the durability of that structure and to the effectiveness with which it would serve its purposes of promoting the general welfare and securing "the blessings of liberty to ourselves and our posterity." [1] These men were convinced that their experiment with free political institutions would fail if the state neglected to cultivate in youth that degree of social understanding and critical-mindedness necessary to judge public issues intelligently.

Thomas Jefferson, writing to James Madison from France in 1787, said: "Above all things, I hope the education of the common people will be attended to; convinced that on this good sense we may rely with the utmost security for the preservation of a due sense of liberty." [2] To Colonel Yancy in 1816 Jefferson wrote: "There is no safe deposit (for the functions of government) but with the people themselves; nor can they be safe with them without information." [3]

George Washington, in his Farewell Address to the American people, said: "Promote, then, as an object of primary importance, institutions for the general diffusion of knowledge. In proportion as the structure of a government gives force to public opinion, it is essential that public opinion should be enlightened."

The feeling of the American people with regard to the civic function of education in the democratic state, and with regard to the relation of the state to education was especially well

[1] Constitution of the United States. *Preamble.*
[2] Quoted by Ellwood Cubberley in *A Brief History of Education,* p. 525. 1922.
[3] *Ibid.,* p. 526.

stated by the Supreme Court of New Hampshire in 1906 in an opinion representative of the courts of practically every state:

The primary purpose of the maintenance of the common school system is the promotion of the general intelligence of the people constituting the body politic and thereby to increase the usefulness and efficiency of the citizens, upon which the government of society depends. Free schooling furnished by the state is not so much a right granted to pupils as a duty imposed upon them for the public good. If they do not voluntarily attend the schools provided for them, they may be compelled to do so. While most people regard the public schools as the means of great personal advantage to the pupils, the fact is too often overlooked that they are governmental means of protecting the state from the consequences of an ignorant and incompetent citizenship.[4]

To a considerable extent the American people have recognized the need for providing opportunity for public education. Today about twenty-six million pupils are enrolled each year in the public elementary and secondary schools of the United States. Approximately 75 per cent of our children of secondary school age are attending secondary schools. We are spending annually about two billion dollars on the education of our children, representing a charge of about $16.00 a year for each person in our total population. It might seem, then, that Jefferson's hope "that the education of the common man will be attended to," has in good measure been realized and that Washington's plea to promote "institutions for the general diffusion of knowledge," has been heeded. Unfortunately, however, the desired result of these educational efforts —the development of an enlightened and competent citizenry —has not been adequately realized.

One hundred and fifty years of public education in the United States have resulted in a generally literate electorate. The great majority of our citizens can read and write on at least an elementary level. And in view of the large numbers of non-English speaking and non-educated peoples who have come to our shores to find refuge and opportunity, this is no

[4] Quoted by Newton Edwards in *Equal Educational Opportunity for Youth,* p. 2. 1939.

mean accomplishment. Our public education has not resulted, however, in the development of a sufficient proportion of citizens who can evaluate critically *what* they read. As Donald DuShane pointed out in his speech as outgoing President at the 1941 convention of the National Education Association, "Over 18,000,000 adults in our population today cannot read a newspaper understandingly or write a simple letter."

Many of these 18,000,000 adults may be able to earn a living for themselves and their families. They may be kind and stable people; they may be good neighbors. But they are not likely to be good citizens. For good citizenship in a representative democracy is not just a matter of keeping within the law and being a good fellow and a kind neighbor. In addition good citizenship calls for the attainment of a working understanding of our social, political, and economic arrangements, and for the ability to think critically about issues concerning which there may be an honest (or even a dishonest) difference of opinion. It calls also for a conviction of the worth of democratic values and ideals such as those embodied in the Constitution of the United States, a kind of conviction which operates to make one willing to put forth serious effort to preserve and extend those values. Functionally illiterate persons, therefore, are not likely to be good citizens in our present complex society.

The experimental study of the development of ability to think critically which is reported in this volume is concerned with a much larger problem, namely, the problem of how to educate more effectively for responsible, competent citizenship which is likely to contribute to the preservation and progressive development of our representative democracy.

DEFINITION OF CRITICAL THINKING

The ability to think critically, as conceived in this volume, involves three things: (1) an attitude of being disposed to consider in a thoughtful way the problems and subjects that come within the range of one's experiences, (2) knowledge of the methods of logical inquiry and reasoning, and (3) some skill in applying those methods. Critical thinking calls for a persistent effort to examine any belief or supposed form of knowledge in the light of the evidence that supports it and the further conclusions to which it tends. It also generally requires ability to recognize problems, to find workable means for meeting those problems, to gather and marshal pertinent information, to recognize unstated assumptions and values, to comprehend and use language with accuracy, clarity, and discrimination, to interpret data, to appraise evidence and evaluate arguments, to recognize the existence (or non-existence) of logical relationships between propositions, to draw warranted conclusions and generalizations, to put to test the conclusions and generalizations at which one arrives, to reconstruct one's patterns of beliefs on the basis of wider experience, and to render accurate judgments about specific things and qualities in everyday life.

The development of ability to think critically, it should be noted, is not limited to cultivation of better methods for finding and testing evidence and meanings, and arriving at well-founded conclusions. Knowledge of the methods of logical inquiry is important. Even more important for the everyday practice of democracy, however, are the *attitudes* involved in critical thinking. Persons who have acquired a disposition to *want* evidence for beliefs, and who have acquired an attitude of reasonableness have also acquired something of a way of life which makes for more considerate and humane relationships among men.

CRITICAL THINKING AS AN EDUCATIONAL OBJECTIVE

The ability to reason logically and to think clearly has long been recognized by some educational leaders as a desirable and most important educational objective. In 1690, for example, John Locke wrote:

So much as we ourselves consider and comprehend of truth and reason, so much we possess of real and true knowledge. The floating of other men's opinion in our brains makes us not one jot the more knowing though they happen to be true. What in them was science is in us but opinionatrety, whilst we give up our assent only to revered names, and do not, as they did, employ our own reason to understand those truths which gave them reputation.[5]

Horace Mann, in his lecture on Education delivered in 1840, said:

Education is to inspire the love of truth as the supremest good, and to clarify the vision of the intellect to discern it. We want a generation of men above deciding great and eternal principles upon narrow and selfish grounds. Our advanced state of civilization has evolved many complicated questions respecting social duties. We want a generation of men capable of taking up these complex questions, and of turning all sides of them toward the sun, and of examining them by the white light of reason, and not under the false colors which sophistry may throw upon them.[6]

More recently bulletins issued by state and county boards of education outlining their educational aims often have included mention of the development of a "scientific attitude," or "the power to think clearly," or "skill in problem solving," or some other aim closely related to what is in this study called critical thinking. Curriculum committees in several states (California, Colorado, New York, and Virginia, for example) and many cities and counties (Bronxville, N. Y., Clayton, Mo., Denver, Colo., Newton, Mass., Norris, Tenn., Pasadena, Calif., Rock Island, Ill., and St. Louis, Mo., for example) in formulating their aims of education have urged emphasis upon the development of critical thinking. To illustrate, the Virginia *Tentative Course of Study for the Elementary School* [7] lists among its Aims of Education "The Attitude of Critical-Mindedness," "The Attitude of Open-Mindedness," and "The Scientific Attitude."

One of the most influential groups in American education, the Educational Policies Commission of the National Education Association, states:

[5] John Locke. *The Educational Writings of John Locke* (I. W. Adamson, Editor), pp. 8–9. Longmans, Green and Co., New York, 1912.

[6] J. E Morgan. *Horace Mann, His Ideas and Ideals,* pp. 93–94. Washington National Home Library Foundation, 1936.

[7] Virginia State Board of Education. *Tentative Course of Study for the Elementary School.* Bulletin No. 5, Vol. XIX, March, 1937.

Critical judgment is developed . . . by long and continuous practice under the criticism of someone qualified to evaluate the decisions. The child must learn the value of evidence. . . . He must learn to defer judgment, to consider motives, to appraise evidence, to classify it, to array it on one side or the other of his question, and to use it in drawing conclusions. This is not the result of a special course of study, or of a particular part of the educative procedure; it results from every phase of learning and characterizes every step of thinking.[8]

Here and there in given schools groups of teachers or individual teachers are devising materials and working out procedures to guide pupils in developing the ability to think critically.[9] By and large, however, our schools have not made a conscious and well-directed effort toward realizing this educational aim. American education is freely criticized today because the ability to think critically is not well developed among secondary school pupils and even among college graduates. Many "educated" persons jump to conclusions which are not supported by evidence, are unaware of their own contradictory statements, seem unable to keep their wishes from influencing their interpretation of data or evaluation of arguments, and, in general, do not make sufficient conscious and voluntary effort to establish belief upon a firm basis of evidence and rationality. As the Educational Policies Commission observes:

The possible contribution of education to the development of tolerance, reason, and fair play has been clearly demonstrated. That the ordinary school does too little in developing these attitudes may be admitted. The omission represents one of the great areas in which the objectives of education need to be reformulated and re-emphasized.[10]

While a large variety of factors have contributed to the failure of our schools to do a more effective job of developing the attitudes, understanding, and skills involved in critical

[8] Educational Policies Commission, *The Purposes of Education in American Democracy*, p. 35. 1938.

[9] See Educational Policies Commission. *Learning the Ways of Democracy.* 1940.

[10] Educational Policies Commission. *The Purposes of Education in American Democracy*, p. 31. 1938.

thinking, the tendency toward overemphasis upon requiring pupils to memorize information and facts deemed important by the teacher should be noted. It is of course true that thinking cannot be carried on in a vacuum; fruitful thinking is dependent upon knowledge. Too often people hold untrue concepts simply because they lack facts and information. There has been too much emphasis in our schools, however, upon feeding students detailed information which has little or no relevance to their needs and lives, and which in large measure they do not assimilate. Too often the procedure has been for the teacher to hand down ready-made generalizations and conclusions rather than to work with the students at problems which have significance for them, helping them to learn how to arrive at generalizations, how to test these generalizations in practice, and how to revise them in the light of new experience. In short, there has been too much concern with having pupils memorize the accepted answers, and not enough concern with guiding them in the processes and methods of arriving at well-found answers.

Symonds, in *Education and the Psychology of Thinking,* develops this point:

Educators have strenuously maintained in book and lecture that one of the aims of the process of education is the development of the power of thought. . . . Education today, notwithstanding the brave assertions of its leaders, does little to cultivate the power of thought. Schools still devote much of their energies to drill and memorization. Most of the training in thinking is really training in following another's thought processes. . . . Education in general is so thoroughly concerned with seeing that pupils get the right answer that the teachers cannot afford to permit pupils to learn to think by permitting them to make mistakes.[11]

The development of critical thinking is a desirable outcome of education not only because it contributes to the intellectual and social competence of the individual and helps him to meet his problems more intelligently and more effectively, but also

[11] Percival M. Symonds. *Education and the Psychology of Thinking,* pp. 3, 13–14. By permission of the publishers, McGraw-Hill Book Company, New York, 1936.

because it helps him to cooperate better with his fellow men. It helps him to form intelligent judgments on public issues and to contribute democratically to the solution of social problems. The author believes that at no time in our history has wider realization of this educational objective been more urgently needed.

THE PROBLEMS OF THIS STUDY

The chief problems of this study are:

1. To develop and present materials and illustrative teaching procedures which may be used effectively by the teacher of upper-grade elementary, secondary, and college students to cultivate a spirit of inquiry and to stimulate growth in ability to think critically.

2. To evaluate the effectiveness of these materials and teaching procedures.

3. To ascertain whether or not there is a relationship between ability to think critically and certain other factors such as intelligence, reading ability, patterns of interest-values, home background, and sex, and to determine whether these factors are significantly associated with amount of gain on the critical thinking tests after receiving special instruction in critical thinking.

Problem (1)—to develop and present materials and illustrative teaching procedures which may be used effectively by the teacher of upper-grade elementary, secondary, and college students to stimulate growth in ability to think critically—includes a subsidiary aim: (a) to describe and illustrate the kinds of behavior which might justifiably be associated with, or be indicative of, the ability to think critically.

Problem (2)—to evaluate the effectiveness of the materials and teaching procedures to stimulate growth in ability to think critically—includes the following aims: (a) to develop valid and reliable instruments to measure some important aspects of the ability to think critically; (b) to ascertain whether the students in the experimental groups, that is, those who have had special training of the kind suggested

in the specially developed lesson units,[12] give evidence (as
determined by a comparison of initial and final test scores)
of greater growth in ability to think critically than those
students in the control groups, that is, those of comparable
age, grade, and mental ability who have had no special training; (c) to determine whether there is a relationship between
teachers' ratings of students' behavior, and students' scores on
the critical thinking tests; (d) to obtain for purposes of
evaluation, some of the opinions and feelings of the students
in the experimental group with reference to the special training
they received in critical thinking; (e) to obtain evidence with
regard to the relative permanence of any improvement which
might be manifested by the experimental group over the
control group in terms of scores on the critical thinking tests.

Problem (3)—to ascertain whether or not there is a relationship between critical thinking and certain other factors—
includes several associated aims: (a) to ascertain whether
there is a relationship between ability to think critically [13]
and reading ability,[14] the individual's pattern of interest-
values,[15] level of general mental ability or intelligence,[16] the
socio-economic status of home background,[17] and feelings of
emotional satisfaction or dissatisfaction; [18] (b) to ascertain
the relative difficulty of reasoning problems dealing with controversial social issues as compared with structurally similar
problems dealing with more abstract and less controversial
issues; (c) to ascertain whether those who scored relatively
high on the critical thinking tests (the top 27 per cent of the
distribution) and those who scored relatively low (the bottom
27 per cent of the distribution) were distinguished by differences in score on any of the other tests used; (d) to ascertain
whether those in the experimental groups who gained the

[12] Eight lesson units were developed and used as instructional materials with
the experimental group. These units are described in detail in Chapter III.
[13] As measured by the Watson-Glaser Tests of Critical Thinking.
[14] As measured by the Nelson-Denny Reading Test.
[15] As measured by the Maller-Glaser Interest-Values Inventory.
[16] As measured by the Otis Quick-Scoring Mental Ability Tests.
[17] As measured by a rating sheet devised by the author.
[18] As measured by Part V of the Maller-Glaser Interest-Values Inventory.

most on the critical thinking tests (the top 27 per cent of the distribution of gains) after the special instruction, and those who gained the least (the bottom 27 per cent of the distribution of gains) were distinguished by differences in score on any of the other tests used.

NATURE OF ASSUMPTIONS AND RESEARCH FINDINGS FROM WHICH THIS STUDY PROCEEDS

The major assumptions made in this study are based upon experimental evidence reported in the literature or upon the author's analysis of the nature and needs of a democratic state. These assumptions and their justifications are stated as follows:

1. In a democracy, it is of vital importance to educate citizens to think critically. The first part of this chapter is devoted to the support and justification of this assumption.

2. The ability to think critically, or at least important aspects of that ability as herein defined, can be improved by certain kinds of educational experiences. This assumption is supported by the evidence from previous research, cited in Chapter II, for instance, Curtis [72],* Fawcett [99], Hill [128], Parker [225], Perry [229], Salisbury [256], and Teller [228].

3. There are a number of component abilities involved in critical thinking.[19] This assumption is supported by the evidence from previous research, cited in Chapter II; for example, Dewey [82], Downing [87], Hill [128], Jewett [147], Salisbury [256], and Tyler [304].

4. Growth in some of the component abilities assumed to be involved in critical thinking may validly and reliably be measured by means of paper-and-pencil tests of critical thinking. This assumption is supported by the opinions and experimental evidence of Burt [41], Downing [88], Hill [128], Noll [218], Thorndike (I. E. R. Tests of Selective and Rela-

---

* Numbers in brackets refer to titles listed in the bibliography at the end of this volume, pages 181-199.

[19] For a statement of these component abilities, see the definition of critical thinking, pp. 5-6.

tional Thinking), Thurstone [297], Tyler [304], Watson [314], Wrightstone [336], and Zyve [340]; and by inference from the fact that other related kinds of intellectual behavior, such as the ability measured by intelligence tests, can be measured from the expression of it afforded by the pencil-and-paper test situation.

5. The abilities involved in critical thinking [20] are related to, but not identical with, the abilities measured by the commonly used intelligence tests, such as the Otis, Thorndike, Army Alpha, and others. There are two types of supporting evidence for this assumption. One type of evidence is the relatively low correlations (ranging between .17 and .71) found between intelligence and tests devised to measure aspects of critical thinking (Billings [23], Jewett [147], Powers [236], Sells [263], Sinclair and Tolman [271], Tyler [303], and Wilkins [324]).

The second type of supporting evidence is that which indicates that aspects of ability to think critically do improve after periods of instruction of varying lengths of time, while similar improvement is not found in tests of intelligence (Curtis [72], Fawcett [99], Hill [128], Salisbury [256], Tyler [303], and Wrightstone [337]). Completely satisfactory evidence is not yet available to indicate to what extent the gains made on critical thinking tests are retained after the instructional period is completed.

[20] As measured by the Watson-Glaser Tests of Critical Thinking.

A young economist appeared before our department for his preliminary examination for the degree of Doctor of Philosophy. He was asked by a competent economist . . . certain questions about some bygone theories in economics. This young student was a very brilliant fellow, much valued by his teachers, and he replied, "I don't take any stock in those theories." The examiner replied, "Neither do I, but I expect you to know what it is in which you take no stock."

—FREDERICK J. E. WOODBRIDGE

CHAPTER II

Review of Research Related to the Problem

THERE are a large number of studies reported in the literature which bear upon different aspects of the broad problem of the development of thinking and reasoning, and upon development of ability to think critically. The studies reviewed in this chapter consequently are referred to under the following nine headings or aspects of the problem: (1) The Nature of the Thinking Process, (2) Causes of Errors in Thinking, (3) Age and Reasoning Ability, (4) Sex and Reasoning Ability, (5) Reasoning and Learning, (6) Reasoning and Intelligence, (7) Reasoning Ability and Academic Standing, (8) Training to Think Critically and Transfer of Training to Think Critically, and (9) The Measurement of Ability to Think Critically.

Such of the studies as bear upon more than one of the nine headings may be referred to several times. The bibliography lists additional references; the studies reviewed in this chapter are those deemed most pertinent to the problem of the development of ability to think critically.

THE NATURE OF THE THINKING PROCESS

The problem of the nature and details of the thought process and of the mental processes involved in solving a problem is of long-standing philosophical as well as psychological interest. The inquiries herein reported shed some illumination upon the problem and at the same time may suggest avenues for further research.

Strasheim [281] presented a series of ten stories to children between the ages of five and ten. All the stories involved a problem which could be solved by the same general method, that of "tossing" a coin or deciding by chance.

The first story supplied the rule. The stories which followed required the testee to apply the relations he had educed in the previous situation to entirely changed "fundaments" or elements available in the new problem. In the last three stories, the testee had to find fundaments for himself, "either by visualizing the situation, or by recalling various features, qualities, etc., associated with it, or by selecting from such reproducts." For example, in the tenth problem two swimmers wanted to determine by chance which one should return to the boat and which should swim to shore. The story ended with "of course they had no money (they were in the water) so they had to find another way."

Strasheim concludes that in the early stages of education, the relations are apprehended as being more or less specific to the fundaments between which they have been educed, "with the result that they are suitable for future occasions only when the same or similar fundaments occur." In the later stages of education, relations are abstracted from their contact with the fundaments, and, as such, may be widely applied to the most varied fundaments.

In a study in which he used specially devised tests to measure reasoning ability in school children between the ages of seven to fourteen, Burt [40] concludes: "All the elementary mental mechanisms essential to formal reasoning are present . . . by the mental age of seven if not somewhat before. Development consists primarily in an increase in the extent and variety of the subject matter to which those mechanisms can be applied, and in an increase in the precision and elaboration with which those mechanisms can operate. . . . A child's reasoning ability thus appears to be a function of the degree of organic complexity of which his attention is capable."

Hazlitt [122] shows that children observe the same general patterns of reasoning as adults, but their ability to render explicit all the implications of the concepts they arrive at comes only rather slowly with age.

Moore [203] found that it was not until the age of ten or eleven that the average child was able to pick out the error in 50 per cent or more of his simple logical fallacies.

Piaget [232] demonstrated that childish thought is egocentric, and suggests that logical reasoning develops in connection with the "socialization" of language and thought. As the child grows older he learns to think and speak partly at least for the benefit of others. He is often called upon to explain and justify his statements, beliefs, and even actions. This is likely to turn his attention to the logical background of his thinking and toward the widely accepted generalizations which make his particular statement or act appear reasonable in the eyes of others.

In his book entitled *How We Think,* Dewey [82] states that the origin of thinking is a felt difficulty, state of doubt, or perplexity.

Given a difficulty, the next step is suggestion of some way out—the formation of some tentative plan or project, the entertaining of some theory that will account for the peculiarities in question, the consideration of some solution for the problem. The data at hand cannot supply the solution; they can only suggest it. What, then, are the sources of the suggestion? Clearly, past experience and a fund of relevant knowledge at one's command. If the person had some acquaintance with similar situations, if he had dealt with material of the same sort before, suggestions more or less apt and helpful will arise. But unless there has been some analogous experience, confusion remains. Even when a child (or a grown-up) has a problem, it is wholly futile to urge him to think when he has no prior experiences that involve some of the same conditions.[1]

Dewey distinguishes between ordinary thinking and reflective thinking (the latter includes "a conscious and voluntary effort to establish belief upon a firm basis of evidence and rationality").

There may . . . be a state of perplexity and also previous experience out of which suggestions emerge, and yet thinking need not be reflective. For the person may not be sufficiently *critical* about the ideas that

---

[1] John Dewey. *How We Think,* p. 15. By permission of the publishers, D. C. Heath and Company, New York, 1933.

occur to him. He may jump at a conclusion without weighing the grounds on which it rests; he may forego or unduly shorten the act of hunting, inquiring; he may take the first "answer" or solution that comes to him because of mental sloth, torpor, impatience to get something settled.[2]

The five phases, or aspects, of reflective thought, according to Dewey, are:

(1) *Suggestions,* in which the mind leaps forward to a possible solution; (2) an intellectualization of the difficulty or perplexity that has been *felt* (directly experienced) into a *problem* to be solved, a question for which the answer must be sought; (3) the use of one suggestion after another as a leading idea, or *hypothesis,* to initiate and guide observation and other operations in collection of factual material; (4) the mental elaboration of the idea or supposition as an idea or supposition (*reasoning,* in the sense in which reasoning is a part, not the whole, of inference); and (5) testing the hypothesis by overt or imaginative action.[3]

Fully as important as Dewey's contribution to the mechanics of the thinking process is his recognition of its dynamics. Thought is instrumental, Dewey points out, and the purposes and desires of the thinker must be kept central in any attempt to understand thinking. Numerous clinical psychologists and psychiatrists have contributed evidence that wishes and unconscious desires play a very important role in steering the thinking process.

In order to discover the mental processes which are required in different types of thought processes, Symonds [286] met with a group of interested and willing graduate students in education for one evening a week during the greater part of a school year. At each meeting he tried to stimulate by appropriate questions one type of mental process (such as selective recall, formulation of a definition, and seventeen other thought processes, each of which Symonds regards as a single aspect of thought). The group was advised that each member would be asked in turn what mental processes he went through in order to reach his solution. Symonds says:

[2] *Ibid.,* p. 16.
[3] *Ibid.,* p. 107.

Out of this more or less introspective form of analysis, several interesting observations were made. In the first place, we are all very dependent on previous experience in the solution of any problem. . . . Another factor in problem solving which this analysis seems to discover is the importance of the concept. The words in the problem as verbally stated and the meaning which they naturally convey are the starting point for the solution. Each word brings up its own trend of associations and the processes of analysis and selection immediately start to operate. With meager concepts, one is limited to the actual concrete association which has been previously made in experience. With more adequate concepts, which have been freed from their concomitants, thinking is more free and versatile.[4]

When the analysis "of each of these separate mental processes was completed," Symonds found that there "seemed to be an interpenetration of mental processes in thinking at all levels, which did not permit one to say that this process was more elementary than that. . . . Certain processes, like *analysis, selection, generalization,* and *organization* seem to occur frequently, suggesting that most processes of reasoning depend on these fundamental operations."[5]

Symonds believes that thinking is a complex act capable of being divisible into components, and that each of these components is a matter of skill and learning in itself, and finally he suggests that the operations of thought conveniently fall into the following classification and that the complete act of thought is an organization of very separate abilities:

    I. Fundamental Psychological Processes
    II. Concepts
    III. Organization of Concepts
    IV. Judgment
        A. Judgments of Fact
        B. Judgments of Value
        C. Evaluation
    V. Organization of Judgments
    VI. Syllogistic Reasoning
    VII. Argument—The Organization of Syllogisms

[4] Percival M. Symonds. *Education and the Psychology of Thinking,* p. 12. By permission of the publishers, McGraw-Hill Book Company, New York, 1936.
[5] *Ibid.,* p. 13.

Commins [68] observes that "the occasion for thought is commonly a new situation dissimilar in some respect to the old. Or it may be that the new situation is not very different, but the available organization has not been retained in a detailed, workable form. Thus, if we forget the actual steps for extracting a square root, we may yet be thinking of the principle involved to reconstruct them." [6] Commins also suggests that:

Earlier schemes of organization (of experiences) become most readily available through *abstraction* and *generalization,* the two distinctive features of thought. . . . Under the guidance of dynamic integrative tendencies, new properties and relationships appear in objects in the perceptual field. . . . The development of thought is a matter of fitting unconnected facts into generalized schemes of understanding. This is comprehension.

It is only when the difficulty is rather clearly defined and when this is seen as fitting into a particular background that the individual undertakes directive thinking. . . . The results of previous trends of development are borne in general "attitudes," "mental sets," "determining tendencies," which manifest themselves as general forms of readiness to think in certain ways or along certain lines. [7]

In an analysis of the trend of human thinking as revealed by language usage, Judd [149] arrives at the conclusion that "active thinking tends in the direction of synthesis of ideas. The mind does not dwell on isolated items of experience but combines these items into integrated systems."

Maier [184, 185] contends that "the term reasoning implies that something new has been brought about and that, in some way, past experiences have been manipulated." He postulates two distinct abilities, reasoning and learning. According to Maier, learning involves the association of contiguous experiences; repetition is necessary for the relationship to be established. Reasoning, on the other hand, is a reorganization of isolated experiences in terms of a goal. These integrations "arise without previous experience and conse-

---

[6] W. D. Commins. *Principles of Educational Psychology,* p. 469. By permission of the publishers, Ronald Press Company, New York, 1937.

[7] *Ibid.,* pp. 470, 501, 502.

quently are new. They are not the product of trial and error."

Duncker [90] agrees with Maier in noting the importance of the subject's seeing in the problem the correct difficulty to be overcome. In agreement with Dewey, Duncker finds that the most common type of solution to a practical problem is that of first seeing the nature of the difficulty to be overcome and then casting about for some means to overcome it. A less common type is that of surveying the available material and from it deriving the appropriate method of solution. This latter approach Duncker found to be common in solving mathematical problems.

Claparède [59, 60] employed problem materials such as skeleton words to be completed, comic pictures for which the subject had to find a title, riddles, and hidden pictures. The problem situation as perceived by the subject aroused a "question" or "need." He believed that a hypothesis might occur to the subject by simple comprehension of the demands of the situation, as in such relatively simple problems as skeleton words, and found that if the hypothesis did not occur immediately trial and error behavior occurred. He concludes that chance may play an important part in the solution of the problem but the solving process is steered throughout by the "question" or "need." The "need" exercises selective action upon the elements present and utilizes those which harmonize with it.

Downing [87] devised a test (described on pages 49-50 of this chapter) "to measure skill in the use of some of the elements and safeguards of scientific thinking." This test was given to over a thousand students in each of the grades eight to twelve and to college freshmen in science classes. On the basis of the mean test scores for the various grades, Downing concludes that "it would appear from those results that ability to think scientifically is a complex of a number of component abilities and that these abilities develop at varying rates, and differently in different communities."

Strauss [282] utilized the test prepared by Downing and ascertained and reported the percentage of pupils, in grades eight to twelve, who made errors or very slight errors in their responses to each of the fifteen parts of the test. Strauss reports:

> The ability to recognize a problem, the ability to observe (i.e. two of the first steps in the thinking process) seem to be the best mastered of the elements studied. On the other hand, the ability to reason, to analyze, and to see essential relationships seem to be the least developed of these processes.[8]

Heidbreder's [124] experiment set the task of discovering the scheme of relations in connection with the placing of geometrical figures in various combinations. She stresses the need of "participant behavior," that is, an attitude of activity toward the problem, manifested by calling up various hypotheses as possible solutions, as "the one activity indispensable to the solution of a problem." She also concludes that "this experiment reveals the importance of successful experience. It shows that concrete successes, occurring in the course of an unsolved problem, have a certain advantage over failure as stimuli to thought."

Confirming Heidbreder's findings, Updegraff and Keister [308] show how a series of successes may transform a child from an attitude of inferiority, inadequacy, evasion, dependence, and regression to an attitude of confident and courageous approach to unfamiliar problems.

Ruger [255] calls attention to the "problem-attitude" as opposed to self-conscious and suggestible attitudes, and indicates the greater effectiveness of the former.

Apropos of the effect of established mental patterns upon the learning of new patterns, Gengerelli [107] has shown that after we have learned to conceive of or react to a thing in one way, it is relatively more difficult to conceive of or react to it in a different way than if the first way had not been learned at all.

Wilhelm [322] investigated the effects of instructions upon syllogistic reasoning and, like Claparède, found that subjects

---

[8] S. Strauss. "Some Results for the Test of Scientific Thinking." *Scientific Monthly*, Vol. 14, pp. 234–252, 1922.

draw inferences from premises only when they have a set to do so. A set to draw inferences may also carry over from one situation to another in which no such instructions are given. Siipola [268] has also found that under certain conditions a set may carry over spontaneously to a subsequent task.

Summary of Studies Concerning the Nature of the Thinking Process

The studies concerning the nature of the thinking process indicate that, while the elementary mental mechanisms essential to formal reasoning are usually present by about the mental age of seven, they are undeveloped at that age. In the early stages of education the child apprehends relations between things as being more or less specific to the particular things between which the relations have been inferred, and as a consequence the apprehended relations are suitable for future occasions only when the same or similar elements occur. In later stages of education, relations are abstracted into guiding principles or generalizations and thus become more widely applicable; unconnected facts come to be fitted into generalized schemes of understanding.[9] This is comprehension. (Strassheim, Commins) The ability to render explicit the implications of the concepts children arrive at comes only rather slowly with age.

The development of logical reasoning is aided through the process of "socialization" as the child often finds it necessary to justify his statements, beliefs, and even actions to other persons (Piaget).

Thinking of a problem-solving kind originates in a felt difficulty, state of doubt, or perplexity (Dewey, Duncker, Claparède, Commins, Wilhelm), and the way this difficulty is apprehended or defined limits the kind of answers that will occur to the thinker. To get out of the rut requires a reformulation of the issue.

[9] Specific classroom procedures found useful for developing skill in applying the principles of logical reasoning to the solution of problems which are of significance to students are described in those references in the bibliography which are marked with an asterisk.

The thinking process may be thought of as reorganization of isolated experiences in terms of a goal (Maier). It is futile, however, to urge a person to do thinking of the problem-solving kind when he has had no prior experiences that involve some of the same conditions (Dewey). If the problem is stated verbally the meaning which the words convey is the starting point for the solution. Each word brings up its own trend of associations and the process of analysis and selection immediately starts. The interpretation of the language by the individual thus influences in a very significant and important way the individual's thinking (Claparède, Dewey, Duncker, Symonds).

The purposes of the thinker, and his wishes and unconscious desires play an important part in steering the thinking process. Furthermore, a feeling of success has been demonstrated to be a potent factor in encouraging a confident and courageous approach to unfamiliar problems (Heidbreder, Updegraff, and Keister).

CAUSES OF ERRORS IN THINKING

Although there is not yet available any complete theory of causes of errors in thinking, various hypotheses have been offered.

Mill [196] divides all errors in thinking into a few distinguishable classes of fallacy: (1) Fallacies of simple inspection, or *a priori* fallacies; for example, the tacit assumption that the same order obtains among the objects of nature as among our ideas of them—that if we always think of two things together, the two things must exist together, i. e., the popular superstition, "Talk of the devil and he will appear." (2) Fallacies of observation; for example, failure to note negative evidence, i. e., undue credit is sometimes given to fortune tellers because the favorable cases are noted, and the others forgotten. (3) Fallacies of generalization; for example, assuming that because a thing is true of some members of a class it therefore is true of all members of that class, i.e., "No woman can drive an automobile competently." (4) Fallacies of confusion; for example, vagueness in language and ambiguity of terms, i. e., "What we need is a good, sound, business government."

Bain [9] adds to this list fallacies induced by (1) the influence of people's feelings, such as self-interest, sympathy, antagonism, love, fear, (2) the influence of associations and habitual modes of thinking, (3) false analogies, and (4) logical errors such as the fallacy of not recognizing plurality of causes.

Shaffer [266] made a study of children's errors in interpreting cartoons. He reports causes of errors similar to those reported by Thorndike [295], and Dewey [82], who report that errors are often induced by faulty understanding of word elements, by the over-potency or under-potency of some elements of the situation in calling out the response, by failure to combine the elements of the situation into appropriate patterns, and by the tendency to react associatively to an inadequate cue, thus supplying the remainder of a pattern imaginatively and without regard to context.

Piaget [232] believes that the young child's tendency to see relationships only in terms of himself and his inability to appreciate objective relationships result in much disconnectedness in his thinking. Piaget also notes that the lack of experience which is needed for understanding often results in errors of thinking.

Huang [134] compared adult and childish thinking by having his subjects explain descriptions of conjurer's tricks and optical illusions. He concludes that Piaget's observation that much disconnectedness in children's thinking arises out of the child's egocentric tendency is overdrawn. Huang believes that simple lack of information accounts for many children's as well as many adult's errors.

Abel [1] tried to gain insight into how people think by having one college student explain something to another. One student listened to a passage or paragraph and attempted to explain it to another student. Abel found that a frequent cause of error appeared to be a tendency to read one's own beliefs and prejudices into the interpretation of that which one seeks to understand and explain.

Maier [181, 184, 186] has suggested that many errors may be due to the inflexibility of the reasoner's set—the tendency of an habitual orientation to block the correct response. Rees and Israel [244] and Claparède [59, 60] have also noted the interfering effect of a rigid set.

Duncker [90], Devnich [80], and Chant [52] reached hypotheses similar to Maier's. They believe that previously conceived relationships to a given material (or situation) will persist and prevent the viewing of the material (or situation) in terms of new relationships, thus keeping the subject from gaining the solution to the problem. Temporary physiological and emotional conditions, such as illness, excessive thirst, hunger, fatigue, and fear or rage, may interfere with thinking at any given time and be responsible not only for straying attention, but also for various types of errors (Cannon [47], James [143], and Woodworth [330]). If the material or the situation is not appropriate to the intelligence or educational level of the subject or is outside the subject's comprehension, inappropriate behavior with the introduction of many types of errors results in a number of instances (Pintner [231], Terman [289]).

Misunderstanding of directions also accounts for a certain proportion of errors in some situations. Such misunderstanding may occur because of lack of attention, interference of a previous frame of reference or set, lack of competence in the language used, ambiguity of terms employed, or sometimes because of such a simple interfering factor as the poor enunciation of the person giving the directions.

Symonds [286] believes that the first step in solving a problem is that of isolating and defining the values operating in the situation, and a possible explanation for failure may be failure to isolate and define the values sought.

Many errors in everyday thinking are due to our failure to consider all the data. We are especially likely to neglect data that do not fit our theories.

Summary of Studies Concerning Causes of Errors
  in Thinking

Causes of errors in thinking may be briefly reviewed: the over-potency or under-potency of some elements in the situation in calling out the response; the effect of temporary or chronic physiological or emotional conditions; material inappropriate to the intellectual or educational level or the experiential background of the individual concerned; the interference of an inflexible set or habitual orientation to a situation (or given material) which prevents the viewing of the situation (or material) in terms of new relationships; faulty language comprehension, or lack of attention, leading to incorrect concept formation or perception of the problem; the influence of wishes, prejudices, and unconscious desires in steering the thinking process; failure to combine the elements of the situation into appropriate patterns; logical errors, such as making false assumptions, false observations, drawing unwarranted generalizations, making false analogies and accepting uncritically the assertions and conclusions advanced by others; lack of order and system in thinking; and failure to isolate and define the values operating in the situation. In general, errors result from aberrations of analysis, selection, association, inference, generalization, and language comprehension.

AGE AND REASONING ABILITY

Gibson and McGarvey [110] present a valuable summary of a number of studies concerning the relationship between age and reasoning ability:

The studies of problem-solving in pre-school children (e.g. Alpert [4], Harter [110], Matheson [193], and Roberts [252, 253]), all report that there is some relationship between age, especially mental age, and achievement. The correlations of achievement with mental age range from + .27 to + .42, but the tendency for a positive relationship is uniformly found. Maier [183] concluded from his experiments that reasoning ability, as he defines it, matures later than learning ability; its time of appearance varies with the child and is related to mental age. Heidbreder's [124] results offer further evidence that problem-solving ability increases with age. Her subjects included groups of children from 2½ to 10 years of age and a group of adults. An interesting feature of her study lies in the analysis made of reasons given for the choice made in multiple-choice situations. Although there was considerable overlapping, the distribution of reasons formed, in general, a "maturity scale."

Extensive investigations of syllogistic reasoning in children from 7 to 17 years of age have been made by Muller [205]. The greatest increases in the ability to make inferences were found between the first and second and the second and third school years. Muller also found that the tendency to imagine concrete situations to represent the premises diminishes with increasing age.

Sells [263] studied the relation of age to scores on his syllogism test (administered as a power test) in a group of adults ranging from 20 to 70 years of age. No relationship of age to test score was found; the correlation obtained was —.20.[10]

Peterson [230] made a study of 577 children in grades five through twelve to measure the ability to solve problems involving a general principle. He concludes: "There is no relation between age and the ability to solve problems involving a general principle when grade in school is held constant, either indirectly by means of the partial correlation technique, or directly by computing the correlation between age and the weight problem scores for each grade."

Strasheim [281] believes his experiments show that in the early stages of education the relations are apprehended as being more or less specific to the elements between which they have been inferred and are as a consequence suitable for future occasions only when the same or similar elements occur. In the later stages of education, the relation is abstracted from its contact with the elements, and, as such, may be widely applied to the most varied situations.

Burt [40] reports that "all the elementary mental mechanisms essential to formal reasoning are present . . . by the mental age of seven, if not somewhat before . . . and then

[10] S. B. Sells. "The Atmosphere Effect: An Experimental Study of Reasoning." *Archives of Psychology*, No. 200, 1936.

development of reasoning appears to consist essentially in an increase in the number, variety, originality, and compactness of the relations which his mind can perceive and integrate into a coherent whole." Burt's findings are confirmed by Jensen [145a] who reports that "Children's thought processes are not qualitatively different from those of adults. As language develops, experience accumulates, and mental age increases, the number and richness of concepts increase correspondingly." Hazlitt's study [122] in general also confirms Burt's conclusions.

Moore [203] found that it was not until the age of ten or eleven that the average child is able to pick out the error in 50 per cent or more of his simple logical fallacies.

Terman and Merrill [290], in the development of the Stanford-Binet Test, found that the average child of seven is able to tell about similarities between such things as wood and coal, a ship and an automobile; and an eight-year-old child's understanding of the fitness of things is clear enough for him to detect the absurdity of such a statement "A man said 'I read in the paper that the police fired two shots at a man. The first shot killed him, but the second did not hurt him much.' " At eleven the average child can state the similarity between such things as wool, cotton, and leather.

Piaget's studies [231, 232] have led him to believe that logical reasoning develops in connection with the socialization of language and thought. He believes the thinking of young children is egocentric in character. For instance, young children have considerable difficulty with the word "because." They find it much easier to distinguish and educe the relation of personal motives for action than to distinguish and educe the cause-effect relation of external events. However, Huang [134], as noted in the section on Causes of Errors in Thinking, believes Piaget's observation concerning egocentricity in young children is overdrawn and that a simple lack of information accounts for many errors made not only by children but by adults.

Maller and Lundeen [188] report a negative correlation of

—.27 between age and superstitious belief among students in grades seven to twelve.

Croxton [70a] tested children from kindergarten age through the eighth grade for their ability to generalize and apply the results of special experience. His data indicate that many children in the higher primary, the intermediate, and the junior high school grades are capable of generalizing, but that junior high school pupils are not markedly superior to intermediate grade pupils in their ability to generalize.

Campbell [45] studied the prejudiced thinking of elementary, junior, and senior high school students by administering a test containing broad general statements about groups of people, such as the Irish, Russians, and Negroes. The statements were all-inclusive, allowing for no exceptions within the group, but provision was made for the response of a pupil who refused to overgeneralize. Among the results reported were the findings that 81 per cent of the statements were prejudiced on the elementary level, and 79 per cent on the senior high school level. Increase in age (and information) did not contribute appreciably to the development of critical thinking as indicated by an unwillingness to make sweeping and unfounded generalizations. This finding tends to show that there is no sound reason for the assumption of incidental transfer from the accumulation of information to the use of information. "There is a crying need," says Campbell, "for specific subject matter and scientific technique for teaching the art of valid thinking."

Similarly, Whittaker [320], in a study of the attitudes of children in the seventh through the twelfth grades toward current political and economic problems, reports: "There was little evidence that the pupils studied became more open-minded from grade to grade. Twelfth grade pupils were only slightly less likely to subscribe to extreme statements than those of the seventh grade."

Studies such as Campbell's and Whittaker's show that under certain kinds of educational training, such as the kind given in the schools attended by the subjects who participated in the

experiments, appreciable improvement in certain aspects of
critical thinking is not manifested simply because the pupils
grow older and more mature. This does not necessarily imply,
however, that a difference in maturity would not make a
difference in the quality of reasoning in the aspects measured
if the pupil's education is pointed toward the development of
the ability to think critically.

Scott and Myers [261] investigated the interpretations of
common terms in history and geography by 173 pupils in
grades five, six, seven, and eight. They concluded that "children have very vague and incorrect notions of some of the
terms frequently used by them in their routine procedure
(terms like 'colonists,' 'taxation,' 'citizen,' etc.). A 'correct'
answer is no proof that the child knows what he has answered."

Stressing the dynamic quality of the development of reasoning ability Commins [68] observes that "the child's progress
in the realm of thought is basically a matter of facilitating the
use of previous schemes of organization in the face of novel
material. These patterns of experience are not born as free-
floating ideas but become available through dispositions which
incline the individual to organize the new material after the
fashion of the old. Nor are they strictly identical from one
occasion to the next, for they themselves undergo the trans-
formations characteristic of development." [11]

Summary of Studies Concerning Age
and Reasoning Ability

There seems to be no necessary positive relationship between mere chronological age and reasoning ability, although
positive correlations (ranging from .27 to .42) are uniformly
found between mental age and achievement (Alpert, Harter,
Matheson, Roberts, Terman). Specific aspects of reasoning as
implied in problem-solving ability do increase with age (Heidbreder), but among children in grades five through ten there
does not seem to be a significant relationship between age and

[11] Commins, *op. cit.*, p. 469.

ability to solve certain kinds of problems involving a general principle (Peterson). The first three school years (approximately between the ages of six and nine) seem to reveal the greatest increase in ability to make inferences (Muller). Among pupils in grades seven through twelve, there is no significant relationship between age and decrease of superstition (Maller and Lundeen), decrease in prejudiced thinking (Campbell), or increase in open-mindedness toward current political and economic problems (Whittaker).

There is no complete agreement as to the precise age at which reasoning ability appears (Burt, Hazlitt, Moore, Piaget, Terman), although there is clear evidence of reasoning ability by the age of seven years.

Children frequently have very vague notions of the terms they use (Scott and Myers). Meaningful, appropriate, enrichment of the experiential background is necessary to promote growth and development of concepts.

An important educational implication of the studies on Age and Reasoning Ability is that training in the development of critical thinking can be begun at a very early age, at least by about seven years.

SEX AND REASONING ABILITY

In analysis of the separate tasks comprising intelligence tests, it has been found that girls are superior in language and boys in mathematical performance. A striking example of this language-mathematical contrast in intelligence test parts appears in the results of the College Entrance Examination Board study reported by Brigham [35]. In all the sub-tests concerned with mathematical problem-solving or concepts, the boys were largely and significantly superior. Where language was a basic element the girls were as largely and significantly in the lead. The difference in favor of the girls on the total verbal score was more than eleven times its standard deviation (in the 1931 report) and the boys' superiority on the total mathematical score was fifteen times its standard deviation. The reports of Wellman [317] and Wooley [334] substantiate Brigham's findings. Hurd [137] suggests that these differences may be more conspicuous on a first testing but may tend to disappear as the sexes are given equivalent training in the functions involved. Hurd's study indicates that these differences between the sexes may be culturally determined rather than native.

Chou, Chen, and Chao [58] gave Thurstone's Reasoning Test B to groups of college students and found that the sex differences in amount of time required to judge a problem and in number of errors were insignificant. The only difference lay in the very slight tendency of men to judge correct conclusions wrong and of women to judge wrong conclusions correct. The authors conclude that the test employed was too easy to differentiate subjects of college age.

Arons [7] found that men were superior to women on a Yerkes multiple-choice problem and believe that this difference was not attributable to a sampling error. Billings [23] used problems from a variety of academic fields and reports that while men ranked but little higher than women on the Army Alpha and on information tests their score on the problems was 48.7 per cent higher than that of the women.

Maier [184, 185], employing both practical mechanical problems and ingenuity problems, found a distinct superiority of men over women. He suggests that the sex differences may be real or that it may mean the problems were better suited to the men. In these experiments Maier also found that the women profited more than the men from suggestions given them to avoid habitual modes of thinking and to look for new methods of attack.

Miles [195] summarizes sex differences in intelligence scores at the college level as follows:

In the parts of tests of intelligence the typical differences that emerged at lower educational levels are here usually more pronounced: they show characteristic mechanical, scientific, problem-solving superiority in the men, linguistic and general verbal superiority in the women. . . . Data available at present show that the lower-scoring sex gains proportionally faster through special practices than the superior sex. This seems to indicate the experiential origin of the initial score difference. Further it appears that interest and experience produce differential rates of learning and contrasts in skill.[12]

Summary of Studies Concerning Sex and Reasoning Ability

The data available on the relation between sex and reasoning ability is to be found largely through analysis of the separate tasks of intelligence tests. The results of these analyses (Brigham, Wellman, Miles) indicate that girls and women are superior in linguistic abilities and verbal expression, whereas boys and men are superior in mathematical, mechanical, scientific, and problem-solving activities. Some studies indicate that these differences may be culturally conditioned, since these abilities can be altered by training (Hurd, Miles).

REASONING AND LEARNING

Maier [183] believes his experiments indicate that reasoning and learning are separate abilities—the former requiring the reorganization of isolated experiences in terms of a goal, and the latter requiring repetition of the experiences in order for the relationship to be established. Billings [23] found correlations ranging from .35 to .59 between information and problem-solving ability in various fields. Arons [7] found no significant correlation between ability to memorize series of playing cards and ability to formulate generalizations in a multiple-choice problem. Ewert and Lambert [98] found a positive correlation between maze-learning and generalizing ability; when full instructions were given in both cases these correlations became significant. Bedell [17] gave paragraphs containing scientific information to pupils in the eighth and ninth grades, and tested factual recall and ability to form inferences from the paragraphs. The results suggest that ability to recall and ability to infer are different but not unrelated.

---

[12] C. C. Miles. "Sex in Social Psychology." *A Handbook of Social Psychology* (C. Murchison, Editor), pp. 737. By permission of the publishers, Clark University Press, Worcester, Mass., 1933.

Commins [68] writing from a Gestalt approach in his chapter on "Learning and Thinking" states:

> An essential feature of learning is the organization of facts into an apprehended whole of experience or behavior. . . . When the child is learning to cut with the scissors, for example, it is the actual steps in the operation itself which are the important things. . . . There are many ends of training which can be served only by preparing the child in advance to meet situations in a rather specific manner. There are many other occasions in life, however, for which the child cannot be specifically prepared beforehand. For such situations as these he can be made ready only in a much more general manner, through the development of comprehensive insights, tendencies, and methods of approach. To make these directly applicable to the problem at hand usually calls for "thinking."
>
> . . . As a special form of learning . . . thinking has its own characteristic features. . . . Thought, instead of being directly concerned with the details of actions or events, as are skill and memory, deals immediately with the scheme or plan or organization which holds these details together. If, in place of actually doing the cutting with the scissors, we direct our attention to the principle of movement according to which the cutting takes place, we are then said to be thinking. . . . Whether thinking plays an important role in learning will depend upon our approach to the field of fact requiring organization.[13]

Summary of Studies Concerning Reasoning and Learning

The evidence suggests that ability to learn and ability to think or reason are not identical but are related. Learning may occur through mere repetition of given experiences, while reasoning appears to require the reorganization of isolated experiences in terms of a goal (Maier).

Reasoning requires a greater degree of intellectual development than mere ability to learn. Critical or reflective thinking involves a higher order of intellectual development, in which the ability to reason is included.

REASONING AND INTELLIGENCE

To the layman the terms reasoning and intelligence are very closely related, if not identical. To the psychologist too it

13 W. D. Commins, *op. cit.*, pp. 468–469.

seems apparent that there is considerable similarity between reasoning, on pencil-and-paper laboratory tests at least, and what is measured on tests of intelligence. What is the character and degree of this relationship?

Billings [23] has a challenging opinion to offer with respect to the status of problem-solving as an ability. He set out to discover whether a person is as good a reasoner in one academic field as another, and gave his subjects problems from such fields as arithmetic, geometry, physics, mechanics, and sociology. Materials necessary for solution were taught the subject first. Correlations between these various fields ran from .53 to .78 and between problem-solving in these fields and Army Alpha the correlations ranged between .42 and .59. He finds that the correlations satisfy the criterion of the tetrad equation, and concludes that problem-solving is a general factor, if not "intelligence" itself.

Sells [263] and Wilkins [324] find significant correlations between syllogistic reasoning and intelligence (.711 and .578), but both find a correlation of the order of .50 between abstract and concrete syllogism scores when intelligence is partialled out. Sells interprets his results as indicating "two separate ability factors, possibly a reasoning factor and an intelligence factor."

Smoke [247] reports a correlation of .52 between speed of concept formation and intelligence. He also notes the use of "hypothesis" in formulating the concept, and the fact that his more intelligent subjects were quicker in abstracting. Ewert and Lambert [98] report correlations ranging from .86 to .96 between various criteria of generalizing and intelligence, and Roslow [254] reports multiple correlations ranging from .32 to .81 between a battery of rational learning problems and various intelligence tests. A multiple-factor analysis of Roslow's results reveals the presence of a common factor in the problems and intelligence tests. Bedell [17] found that students in the lower quartile of their group in intelligence scored scarcely better than chance on an inference test.

Powers [236] correlated scores on a test of common superstitions with scores on the University of Washington Intelligence Examination, and obtained a coefficient of .15. He concludes: "Intelligence does not appear to be a safeguard against credulity or false belief."

Salisbury [256] reports that training in the conscious use of outlining and summarizing material as a method of study results in improvement in reasoning and in reading ability. "The effect of the training on I. Q., however, is not great, such gains as did occur probably being due to improved reading ability."

Sinclair and Tolman [271] report a correlation of .49 between scores on the Thorndike Intelligence Examination and the Inference Test of the Watson test of fairmindedness. Peterson [230] conducted a study with 577 children in grades five through twelve to measure the ability to solve problems involving a general principle (the law of the lever: that a lever is balanced when the weight, x distance on one side, is equal to weight, x distance on the other side). Grade in school gave a higher zero order coefficient (.55) with the weight problem scores than did intelligence test scores with the weight problem scores (.40). On the basis of an analysis of scores of over one thousand students on his Test on Scientific Thinking, Downing [88] states: "The conclusion seems inevitable that general intelligence as expressed by the I. Q. is something quite different from ability to handle either the elements or safeguards of scientific thinking (if these exercises test such ability)."

Jewett [147] experimented with two high school groups, matched for I. Q., reading ability, grade level, and scores on four tests designed to measure the ability to detect and to analyze propaganda. He presented two special units of work on propaganda analysis to the experimental group. After comparing the experimental and control groups on retest scores, Jewett concludes: "A higher relationship exists between knowledge of facts about social problems and ability to detect and analyze propaganda concerning those problems than exists between intelligence and ability to detect propaganda." The correlation in the former instance was .49, in the latter, .17.

In an experiment with fifty parochial school children between twelve and sixteen years of age, Wegrocki [316] attempted to determine the effect of certain propaganda material on responses of "liking" and "hating" to fifty-six words on an "attitude sheet." Wegrocki found "a tendency for the more intelligent to be less influenced by propaganda than the less intelligent."

Osborne [222] used a unit of instruction designed to teach pupils to resist propaganda, and then compared their resistance with control classes which were assigned no work on the subject of propaganda. Among his conclusions, Osborne reports:

. . . The evidence presented by this study indicates that neither achievement nor intelligence, as commonly measured, is a dependable index of ability to resist propaganda. . . . While the possession of knowledge and intelligence is no doubt necessary in order to do critical thinking, the results of this experiment strongly suggest that an individual may, according to commonly obtained measures, possess both these traits to a high degree and yet be highly susceptible to propaganda influences.[14]

Stressing the differences between intelligence and ability to think, Commins [68] states that:

. . . Although intelligence is sometimes defined as the ability to think, the two functions are not really the same. A person's thinking is a reflection of his intelligence plus other factors. While we may measure general mental maturity with very little stress upon knowledge, we cannot estimate the quality of a person's thinking apart from the truthfulness and value of the knowledge he attains in this manner. To think is to think about something, and to think well is to attain true knowledge about this something through the reorganization of experience. Thought is a step closer to knowledge than is intelligence. The teacher may be a better thinker than his student, the old man better than the boy, the urbanite better than the farmer, the high school student better than the savage youth, in spite of very little difference in I. Q.[15]

[14] W. W. Osborne. "Teaching Resistance to Propaganda." *Journal of Experimental Education*, Vol. 8, pp. 1–17, 1939.
[15] Commins, *op. cit.*, p. 499.

*Summary of Studies Concerning Reasoning
   and Intelligence*

Since there is a multiplicity of conceptions of what reasoning and what intelligence signify, and since there are numerous ways of measuring each or both, it is difficult to evaluate their relationship adequately. Some investigators (Billings) believe that problem-solving ability is a general factor if not "intelligence" itself. Most investigators find, however, that while reasoning ability or problem-solving ability is an important part of what we measure by tests of "general intelligence," reasoning ability is not the whole of what we consider to be manifestations of intelligence (Bedell, Sells, Smoke). In any case, intelligence alone does not appear to be a safeguard against credulity or the holding of false and unfounded beliefs. General intelligence as expressed by the I. Q. is something different from ability to reason logically and think critically (Jewett, Osborne, Powers, Salisbury, Sinclair, and Tolman). Ability to reason is subject to improvement upon training, whereas I. Q. does not increase significantly with the same training (Salisbury). As Commins puts it, "An individual's ability to think out a problem at any level of education or scientific achievement will depend upon his general mental maturity, his background of experience, certain character or volitional traits, and his facility in the use of language."

REASONING ABILITY AND ACADEMIC STANDING

Do students who score high on tests of reasoning ability tend to get significantly higher school grades than students who score relatively low in reasoning ability, and do those who receive high grades tend to be superior in their reasoning ability?

Washburn [312] selected 113 students at Vassar on the basis of their ability in mathematics. One group consisting of fifty-four students with marked ability and another group of fifty-nine students with marked lack of ability were given a test in logical reasoning, not mathematical in character. There were twenty arguments (such as: "The express train alone does not stop at this station; and as the last train did not stop, it must have been an express train.") to be answered "sound" or "false." Results were compared with mathematical records and academic records and the conclusions based on comparison of mean scores were as follows: (1) Intellectual ability, as represented by high academic standing, and reasoning ability, as represented by results of tests, are related. (2) High academic standing does not necessarily guarantee good reasoning ability, but good reasoning ability is an excellent guarantee of high academic standing. (3) Poor reasoning ability does not exclude high academic standing but low academic standing excludes good reasoning ability (with one exception in this test). (4) Good reasoning ability guarantees high academic standing more than it guarantees high academic standing plus good mathematical ability. (5) Where academic standing is high, reasoning ability is only a little higher in the group that is good in mathematics than in the group that is good in other subjects only. The ability to reason with mathematical, quantitative relations does not add much to the ability to reason with non-quantitative relations. (6) Mathematical ability may exist without good reasoning ability and with low academic standing. (7) Poor mathematical ability excludes good reasoning more than poor reasoning excludes good mathematical ability.

Summary of Studies Concerning Reasoning Ability and Academic Standing

Washburn's study is the only one found in the literature which deals specifically with the relationship between reasoning ability (as distinguished from general intelligence) and academic standing. The study provides evidence that academic standing and reasoning ability are related, that high academic standing does not ensure good reasoning ability as frequently as good reasoning ability ensures high academic standing, and that poor reasoning ability does not exclude high academic standing but low academic standing definitely tends to exclude good reasoning ability.

TRAINING TO THINK CRITICALLY AND TRANSFER OF TRAINING TO THINK CRITICALLY

Is it possible to develop ability to think critically through providing pupils with given kinds of educational experiences? Can we develop ability to think critically through training?

This study has started with the assumption, justified by the evidence to be presented in this section, that it is possible to develop such ability by means of appropriate education. Before reviewing the experimental evidence, it might be well to note some differences of opinion expressed by a few selected educators who have been seriously concerned with this problem.

Biddle [21] states that:

Skill in tolerant controversy is a learned habit which must be developed over a period of years. The discussion process should start in the first and second grades on subjects within the child's scope of interest.

Broome [36] writes:

The guiding purpose of education is to teach how to think. . . . The school should give greater attention to the development of methods whereby children may be trained in habits of critical judgment.

Carroll [50] writes:

Ability to reason is not due to any special endowment or aptitude, and the study of no one subject will develop this ability. . . . While in general this habit depends upon practice, the ability to reason with reference to a given problem or situation depends upon a knowledge of the elements of the problem or situation.

Powers [237] states that:

Experiments with science groups have shown . . . that students who have been allowed opportunity and encouraged to use initiative and independent thought and action will use these to a greater extent than students who have not had such opportunities.

Boraas [31] writes:

What place is accorded to thinking in our schools of to-day? Several years of experience as a teacher and superintendent have convinced me that real thought exercises are exceedingly rare in ordinary school work. Nearly all the time and effort is spent in memorizing, in repeating what has been memorized, or in acquiring some form of skill by means of mechanical repetition. Occasionally apparent thought questions or thought exercises may occur; but even in these the thinking is done mostly by the teacher. They seldom cause a real perplexity cr involve serious thought on the part of the pupils. . . .

What has become of all the facts that we committed to memory and could repeat acceptably in school examinations? They have deserted by squads, companies, and regiments because they were never called into actual service after inspection day.

The ability to exercise good judgment in regard to affairs of practical life is an important element of successful living and should be emphasized much more than it has been in our schools. Who does most of the judging in the ordinary schools? But will any amount of practice by the teacher develop skill in the pupils? Would any practical teacher of agriculture today expect to develop his students into good judges of corn or stock by doing all the judging himself? There is a crying need for better methods in the development of this type of thinking in connection with the teaching of the ordinary school subjects and the management of school activities generally. . . .

Problem solving must continue to be one of the important aspects of thought training. However, we must develop better methods for securing this training than those which are used in the ordinary school. We must select more vital problems for the pupils to solve. Then, too, we must discover methods for making the pupils consciously clear as to the best methods and means for solving the different types of problems. We must also give our pupils more practice in the solving of long problems, such as will take not only days but weeks and months for their solution. Success in life requires "long-headedness." Most of our school work has been a training for the opposite.

Efficiency in thought requires broadmindedness and ability to exercise criticism. . . . How can this be accomplished? It can be done only by practice in thinking about affairs that involve a large number of considerations which the pupil must judge as to their relative values. It requires practice in dealing with questions and problems about which there are differences of opinion, and in the solution of which success depends on a fair appreciation of such opinions and a tactful adjustment of differences. This means that we must let—no, that is not strong enough—we must require our pupils to think about the large problems

of the school and take a part in carrying forward the general management of the institution.[16]

Wood and Beers [296] take the view that very few out of
the vast majority of students now in high schools and college
can be trained to reason competently and think critically by
any kind of curricula or teaching procedures and that ability
to think critically depends upon one's intelligence and knowledge and respect for facts. They write:

Even in the annual conventions of professional educators one hears
loudly applauded papers which demand that teachers shall make their
pupils think, because the thing that is important is not the "what" but
the "how." This demand is made of all teachers in regard to all pupils,
despite the obvious fact that large proportions of both groups cannot
think, and that many cannot even learn or understand the bare facts
and simple relations connoted by the courses of study. . . .

The whole history of science and thought is a convincing testimonial
of the ineluctable dependence of fruitful thinking on knowledge. . . .

Thinking can have no real existence, and no effective stimulus, apart
from knowledge. Perhaps the best, if not the only, way to promote fruitful thinking is to promote knowledge and a deeply set respect for facts.
If facts of large or small portent cannot provoke a person to thinking,
it is doubtful whether a teacher or anything else can. . . .

The obvious and widely known fact that college graduates are not
educated is not owing to lack of heroic efforts on the part of teachers to
"train" students in pure thinking, but rather to the fact that their
magic, even when learned at the feet of the most notorious leaders of
the thinking cult, is not sufficient to perform the miracle of turning
muscle and proper academic allegiance into cerebral cortex. . . .

Numberless experiments have shown that . . . forgetting (of information) is the rule rather than the exception in American schools. But
such evidence does not impugn the value of knowledge, either intrinsi-
cally or as a basis for fruitful thinking. It merely shows, among other
things, that the pupils have been taught wastefully, and that the curriculum is highly disjointed. . . .

Taken in the large, the weight of the test evidence of the last two
decades is sufficiently consistent to indicate that information and knowledge are at least partly within the control of teaching and that thinking
and thinking ability are certainly much less, if at all, under the control

[16] J. Boraas. *Teaching to Think*, pp. 6, 13, 15. By permission of The Macmillan Company, publishers, New York, 1922.

of teaching, except as thinking can be determined in quality and range of knowledge. . . .

It is fairly obvious that neither facts nor teaching nor exhortations can enable some people to think. There must be both capacity and motivation, and aggressive respect for facts, before fruitful thinking is possible.[17]

One might note here, as Judd does in his *Education as Cultivation of the Higher Mental Processes,* that while fruitful thinking is dependent upon knowledge, the presence of knowledge is certainly not a guarantee that there will be fruitful thinking. The criticism that there has been too much emphasis in education on feeding students isolated facts which they too frequently do not assimilate and make functional is a valid one.[18] Tyler [304], for example, reports:

Interviews with college students indicate that more than 60 per cent of the students in college believe that the chief duty of college students is to memorize the information which their instructors consider important. The emphasis given to the recall of facts in typical college examinations is one of the chief reasons for the existence of this belief. The vast majority of examinations mainly require students to remember and state facts presented in textbooks and lectures. It is not surprising that students think of memorization as the fundamental requirement in education.[19]

Beauchamp [16] asked twenty-six teachers of science in almost as many states, whom he visited in connection with the National Survey of Secondary Education, how they trained pupils to do scientific thinking. The answers were of five types: (1) The study of science results automatically in this ability because of the nature of the subject matter of science. (2) It is not possible to train a pupil to think. (3) We had a lesson on that last week, or we will have a lesson on that next week. (4) We take that up in the introduction to the course.

[17] B. D. Wood and F. S. Beers. "Knowledge versus Thinking." *Teachers College Record,* Vol. 37, pp. 487–499, 1936.

[18] Professor Wood agrees with this criticism. He told the author that his article with Beers was intended primarily as an attack against a movement to disparage acquisition of knowledge, which he considers basic to good thinking.

[19] R. W. Tyler. "Measuring the Results of College Instruction." *Educational Research Bulletin,* Vol. 11, pp. 253–260, Ohio State University, 1932.

(5) The pupils learn the method by watching the procedure of the teacher. None of the answers was sufficiently definite to give the investigator a clear idea of what was being done in this direction. This does not necessarily mean that no training in scientific thinking is being carried on, but it does mean that such training is not being given in a systematic fashion.

Curtis [73] found that junior high school pupils may be trained through general science to develop attitudes of avoidance of narrow-mindedness and of the tendency to hasty inferences. His conclusions are that a little instruction in the elements of scientific attitudes is of great value and that direct, definite training toward this end is more productive of the desired results than extensive training in scientific subject matter, extensive reading in general science, or regular classroom instruction in general science.

Caldwell and Lundeen [44] presented a unit of instruction in unfounded beliefs in science to a high school class in biology. Their results show a decrease in unfounded belief pertaining to such things as weather, climate, health, and character analysis, and an increase in factual knowledge. The change in the former was greater.

Zapf [339] was concerned with two major questions: (1) What is the efficacy of general science in reducing children's superstitions when no emphasis is placed on this? (2) What changes are there in the number of superstitious beliefs held by children following a course in general science directed toward eliminating superstitions?

Six questions were compiled which required the child to state his problem, recall past experiences, form a hypothesis, make a workable plan, search for facts, and weigh his evidence with respect to its pertinence, soundness, and adequacy. At the end of the semester, the 285 ninth grade pupils who had spent two hours each week solving problems in this scientific manner were tested with the Maller and Lundeen superstition test, the Zapf superstition test, and the Woodworth Mathews Personal Data Sheet. Five hundred and sixty-four pupils who had taken the Maller and Lundeen superstition test and whose work had had no special emphasis upon superstitions were retested and their scores were grouped according to the number of semesters of general science work the pupils had had previous to the experiment, and averages of the scores in each group were determined. Among her findings, Zapf reports:

1. Regular general science work seemed to have no effect in reducing superstitious beliefs, the mean number of superstitions held by pupils having had five semesters of general science being 9.64, while those who have had only one semester averaged 9.58.

2. Superstitious responses were definitely decreased following a period of instruction directed toward this.

3. There was a greater decrease in superstitious responses on the Zapf test (10.36) than on the Maller and Lundeen test (5.10) indicating probably that children find it easier to cease saying that a superstition is true than to cease feeling the influence of it.

4. The mean percentage of children who consistently showed belief in the same superstition on both tests was 35.9 per cent before the period of instruction and 25.5 per cent afterward, indicating that the majority of children do not seem to be consistent in their superstitious beliefs.[20]

E. B. Moore [202] reports a study in which she attempted to test the assumption of science teaching at the junior high school level that a scientific attitude is developed by a knowledge of scientific facts and varies directly with such knowledge. Miss Moore constructed two tests: one to measure the amount of factual knowledge possessed with reference to material taken up in junior high school general science courses, and another to measure the ability to select the truest statement from a list of statements applicable to the same situation but differing in accuracy. The judgment test included descriptions of fifty similar situations with four or five possible explanations for each.

The tests were applied to twenty subjects from each of the following groups: (1) eighth grade pupils who had studied no science, (2) ninth grade pupils who were studying general science, (3) junior college students who were studying ad-

[20] R. M. Zapf. "Superstitions of Junior High School Pupils. Part 2, Effect of Instruction on Superstitious Beliefs." *Journal of Educational Research*, Vol. 31, pp. 481–496, 1938.

vanced science, (4) adults who had studied no science, (5) elementary school teachers who had had little or no science, and (6) high school teachers who had had considerable science. Miss Moore's conclusions are:

1. That phase of the scientific attitude which is known as the ability to distinguish a valid explanation for a given situation in daily life from explanations less valid is clearly related to a knowledge of scientific facts and principles.

2. One's ability to apply knowledge is not in direct proportion to one's knowledge of facts. Knowledge may be a result of superficial reading or rote memory, or one may be able to apply effectively a limited knowledge of facts.

3. Other factors tend to influence the relation between a scientific attitude and factual knowledge. (a) The study of science for at least a year increases the proportion of facts which can be applied. (b) The presence of prejudice or of superstition diminishes the degree of application of the facts known. (c) Scientific reading increases both the knowledge of facts and the extent to which that knowledge is applied. (d) Superior intelligence, general educational training, and experience increase the knowledge of facts and the ability to apply that knowledge. (e) Scientific interests stimulate the acquisition of a knowledge of facts but do not appreciably affect the ability to apply that knowledge.

4. Sex differences have little evident effect on the amount of factual knowledge or the ability to apply it.

5. No person is able to apply all the facts he knows. However, when the facts are known, the fewest errors are made in the situations in which a person has had the most experience. It follows, then, that the methods employed in the teaching of science should present facts and principles in relation to as many of the important situations in daily life as possible.[21]

Downing [87] devised a test of some of the elements and safeguards of scientific thinking which he administered to twenty-five hundred pupils from the eighth to twelfth grades inclusive. The scores of students who had studied science for varying lengths of time from zero to four years were compared with and related to intelligence quotients. He concludes: (1) There was no evidence that high school students acquire skill in scientific thinking as a necessary by-product of

[21] E. B. Moore. "A Study of Scientific Attitudes as Related to Factual Knowledge." *School Review*, Vol. 38, pp. 379–386, 1930.

the study of scientific subjects as at present taught. (2) There was an indication of superiority of scores of students who had three to four years of science. Since it has been established that for the most part only students with a relatively high I. Q. take advanced chemistry and physics, Downing concludes that the superiority was not due merely to increased amount of science instruction.

Davis [78] developed two tests, one a cause-and-effect relationship test and the other a fact-theory test to measure scientific attitude. These tests were administered to teachers and pupils in a Wisconsin high school, and from the test results, Davis reports (among other things) the following: (1) High school pupils in these tests make almost as good records as the teachers. (2) Pupils seem to have a fairly clear concept of the cause-and-effect relationship, but they do not seem to be able to recognize the adequacy of a supposed cause to produce the given result. (3) Teachers do not consciously attempt to develop the characteristics of a scientific attitude. If pupils have acquired these characteristics, it has come about by some process of thinking or experience outside the science classroom.

Noll [218] constructed a test which purports to measure each of six habits of scientific thinking (accuracy, suspended judgment, open-mindedness, intellectual honesty, criticalness, and the habit of looking for true cause-and-effect relationships). The preliminary form of the test was given to 383 boys and girls enrolled in grades eight through twelve. The average score on the test increased regularly from the eighth grade to the twelfth and indicated that the thinking of these pupils became more scientific as they went through the high school and as they matured, insofar as the test actually tested scientific thinking. However, the results of the testing show that even the pupils making the highest scores were still inaccurate, hasty, and not always honest in their thinking. They jumped at conclusions and they still had unreasonable prejudices.

In another paper, Noll [219] writes:

A method which emphasized pupil initiative and pupil activity would be useful for developing good habits of thinking provided that they were made the goal of that method. . . . The habits of thinking that were listed as constituting the scientific attitude (in the study previously referred to) should be taught and developed directly as such. The habit of openmindedness and of suspended judgment should be formed by practicing them in our teaching and by helping our students to practice them. Direct definite training toward (the development of the scientific attitude) is more productive of the desired results than extensive training in scientific subject matter, extensive readings in general science, or regular classroom instruction in general science. . . . (4) Practice must be given in the formation of these habits in specific situations. . . . (5) The habits that constitute scientific thinking should be generalized. . . . (6) Opportunities for practice of scientific thinking must be given in all possible situations. . . . (7) The learning of scientific habits of thought must be made meaningful and desirable to the pupils to insure efficiency and permanency of learning. . . . Attainment of the objective (of developing scientific habits) will come when we begin to teach for it. Our teaching at present is for knowledge of facts and principles, not for methods of thinking. Our curriculum, our textbooks, our examinations, the entire teaching organization and purposes are in terms of the accumulation of factual knowledge. Attainment of other objectives will result through placing the emphasis on learning to think rather than learning to recite.[22]

Powers [237] observes that experiments with science groups "have shown . . . that students who have been stimulated to find the wide ramifications of scientific knowledge through their lives will be more cognizant of these ramifications than students who have not been so stimulated; and that students who have been allowed opportunity and encouraged to use initiative and independent thought and action will use these to a greater extent than students who have not had such opportunities."

Sinclair and Tolman [271] attempted to ascertain whether individuals trained in science and mathematics "tend to be more logical, more reasonable, less affected by presuppositions and prejudices when considering common economic, political, social, and religious issues than do others of equal education and experience, but trained generally in liberal arts." Goodwin Watson's test of fair-mindedness [314] was administered to two groups of college students, one from a liberal arts college and one from a school of science and engineering. The mean of liberal arts freshmen in percentage prejudice score significantly exceeded the mean of liberal arts seniors. Sinclair and Tolman say of this finding in favor of the seniors: "This would seem to indicate that three years of liberal arts work was somewhat effective in decreasing the tendency to reach conclusions based upon prejudice." No significant difference was found between the mean of science freshmen and science seniors; but in both cases they were superior to corresponding liberal arts groups, with a large difference between freshmen groups and a significantly smaller difference between senior groups of the two institutions. They conclude:

We have found here no evidence for the "transfer" of logicality or reasonable habits of thoughts from fields of specific scientific training to fields involving questions of economic, ethical, and social judgments as they are presented in the Goodwin Watson test. The results of the study show that there is a correlation between the choice of the scientific vocation and the ability to draw correct inferences. There is, however, no indication that this correlation is to be ascribed to the scientific training itself, and we think it not unreasonable that the pursuit of science should attract a group on the whole superior in this respect.[23]

Daily [75] made a study of the ability of ninth grade pupils to select essential data in algebra problems, when these contained superfluous data, and of their ability to detect deficiencies in problems lacking essential data. His results agree with the findings of Curtis concerning the value of direct instruction in developing critical thinking.

Hall [116] purposely selected students for their lack of ability to do the work in a regular geometry class, and approached the subject with them by showing the need of proof in the students' everyday lives and experiences. The experi-

[23] J. H. Sinclair and R. S. Tolman. "An Attempt to Study the Effect of Scientific Training upon Prejudice and Illogicality of Thought." *Journal of Educational Psychology*, Vol. 35, No. 5, pp. 362–370, 1933.

ences of the pupils were used for illustration in trying to bring about an understanding of the methods of drawing valid conclusions and the concepts of proof as used in geometry. Hall concludes that geometry can be used as an effective and convenient vehicle for teaching the nature of valid inference if the whole structure of geometric applications and life applications are interwoven. "The fact of transfer (of training) from one activity to related activities seems established. But the equally important consideration that in order to obtain this transfer we must teach for it, has not yet received due emphasis."

Lazar [167] developed a method of teaching geometry in such a manner as to encourage generalization and showed how geometry might be utilized "as a medium for making the pupils conscious of the existence of logical patterns of valid and invalid reasoning in mathematics as well as in the thinking of everyday life."

Parker [225] set up a controlled experiment in an effort to answer the question, "Can pupils of geometry be taught to prove theorems more economically and effectively when trained to use consciously a technique of logical thinking; and furthermore, does such training, more than the usual method, increase the pupils' ability to analyze and see relationships in other, non-geometrical, situations?" An experimental and a control group were taught by the same teacher. The pupils in the experimental group studied the thought process used in proving geometric theorems and gained some understanding of the nature of logical thought, while in the control group the theorems themselves were recognized as of major importance and little attention was given to the thought process involved in proving them. The results of the training were measured by giving geometric theorems to the classes before and after their work. Parker concludes:

These data would seem to offer conclusive evidence, insofar as one experiment can be considered to do so, that when pupils are taught to use consciously a technique of logical thinking, they try more varied methods of attack, reject erroneous suggestions more readily, and without becoming discouraged maintain an attitude of suspended judgment until the method has been shown to be correct. The data on the reasoning tests . . . indicate that . . . training in logical thinking . . . tends to carry over these methods of attack and these attitudes . . . to other problem situations.[24]

Perry [229] constructed a special reasoning test by selecting items from several standardized reasoning and intelligence tests, such as the Institute for Educational Research Tests of Generalization and Organization, and of Selective and Relational Thinking, the Burt Graded Reasoning Test, the Terman Group Test of Mental Ability, and others. Two control groups and one experimental group were equated on the basis of scores received on Perry's special composite reasoning test. Each group was composed of three divisions of reasoning ability—average, superior, and very superior. In each control group the instruction was definitely guided by a textbook. In one of these groups, the book propositions were emphasized, while in the other the emphasis was placed on the proving of original exercises. No attention was given in either group to any particular method of thinking and in each case, the class was conducted by the question and answer method. The experimental group was first taught techniques of reasoning such as analysis of facts into their elements, and purposive thinking when formulating and testing possible solutions. Emphasis was placed on the "if—then" type of thinking as well as the analytic method. The techniques learned were then applied to geometry problems. The results showed that the experimental technique markedly helped the average students, was of slight benefit to the superior students, and was detrimental to the very superior group. Perry concludes that the "experimental technique in reasoning was the means of decreasing students' difficulties in the solution of exercises in geometry and it also developed habits which led to successful solutions." Although non-mathematical subject matter was not included in the course, in the experimental group "the ability to solve problems of non-mathematical character was markedly improved,

[24] E. Parker. "Teaching Pupils the Conscious Use of a Technique of Thinking." *The Mathematics Teacher*, Vol. 17, No. 4, pp. 191–201, 1924.

following the period of training in the solution of exercises in geometry. This increased ability was more noticeable as resulting from those tests more nearly similar to the type of reasoning emphasized in demonstrative geometry in form and content."

Shendarker [267] used several different methods in training subjects to solve arithmetic problems and found that the transfer to several reasoning tests was roughly proportional to the degree of similarity between training and test materials. He found no transfer to "general reasoning," as tested by the Burt Graded Reasoning Test.

Fawcett [99] describes classroom procedures (in connection with the teaching of geometry) which might be used as a means for cultivating critical and reflective thought and for evaluating the effect of such procedures on the thinking of the pupils. He investigated three related problems: (1) the problem of leading the pupil to understand the nature of deductive proof through the study of geometric situations, (2) the problem of generalizing this experience so that effective transfer will result, and (3) the problem of evaluating the resulting change in the behavior of the student. His class of twenty-five students met four times a week for a period of two school years. The first four weeks were spent in discussing undefined terms, definitions, and assumptions. Classroom practice centered on the method by which theorems are established. The method of proof was then applied to the analysis of arguments in connection with the fields to which transfer was desired. Editorials, advertisements, political speeches, and court evidence were analyzed for basic assumptions and for the evidence offered in support of the given conclusions. Fawcett reports the following results:

1. Mathematical method illustrated by a small number of theorems yields a control of the subject matter of geometry at least equal to that obtained from the usual formal course. (Determined by administration to the experimental and the control groups of the Every Pupil Plane Geometry Test, published by the State Department of Education at Columbus, Ohio.)

2. By following the (class) procedures (described), it is possible to improve the reflective thinking of secondary school pupils.

3. This improvement in the pupil's ability for reflective thinking is general in character and transfers to a variety of situations.

4. The usual formal course in demonstrative geometry does not improve the reflective thinking of the pupils.[25]

Jones [148] used five of Thurstone's attitude scales to study the attitudes of college students and the changes in such attitudes during four years in college. He concludes that "In order to increase the degree of generality in the attitudes and conduct of students, teachers must direct their education toward generalization, rather than assume that whenever improvement is made in one area it will spread widely by some automatic generalizing process."

Barlow [14] gave an initial and a final test consisting of fifteen Aesop fables to four groups—an experimental and a control group of elementary school pupils, and an experimental and a control group of adults. The task in both initial and final tests was to write the lesson conveyed by each fable. The experimental groups were given twelve carefully planned lessons treating several phases of simple analysis, abstraction, and generalization. The control groups were not given this special training. Barlow concludes from his experiment that when students are given training in abstracting, analyzing, and generalization, a relatively large amount of transfer occurs.

Hill [128] constructed four tests designed to measure ability to see the relationship of evidence. The tests were (1) logic, (2) problematic arithmetic, (3) fables, and (4) situations. The tests were given to five groups each of sixty children between ten and eleven years of age, equated for age and intelligence (on the basis of Spearman's intelligence test). For four weeks each of four groups was trained in a different type of evidential material while the fifth group did not receive special training. All five groups were then tested again. Hill found that specific improvement occurred with all sets

[25] H. P. Fawcett. *The Nature of Proof*. Thirteenth Yearbook, The National Council of Teachers of Mathematics, Bureau of Publications, Teachers College, Columbia University, 1938.

of material and that training in a particular kind of material improves the ability to deal with that material. The improvement obtained by training in reasoning upon logical exercises was not as great as the improvement with the other materials. Hill believes that this may be due to the fact that logic requires more of the general factor in intelligence, whereas the other tests require the development of a *specific* factor. In considering the effects of training with one kind of material on other types she found that training in logic has a negative effect on arithmetic and on fables. Improvement in material dealing with situations was less for the group trained in logical exercises than with groups trained with other types of material. Hill says "A possible explanation of the adverse effect of logical training is that the training in this material may have produced a more cautious and hesitant attitude. It may have created a tendency to examine problems more closely; possibly even making the testee look for a 'catch' and consequently, the performance of the tests was hindered. Additional training, however, might have had the effect of making the testees more sure with a consequent improvement in other tests. If this is the correct solution we have evidence of an attitude being transferred." She concludes that "There is no general increase in ability to reason. There is a specific gain and this gain is not transferable, except in cases where the method of attack facilitates the handling of the new type of material." [26]

It would appear that it is useless to depend on one subject to improve another, for improvement can be obtained only by specific training (except where a method of attack or attitude can be found common to two or more subjects).

Another important finding reported by Hill is that "children who scored low on the initial testing gained more than those who had scored high at the initial testing." Hill challenges Gates' and Van Alstyne's [106] assumption in their experiment that gains are independent of the initial scores.

[26] M. Hill. *Training to Reason*, pp. 23–24, 26. Melbourne University Press, Melbourne, Australia, 1936.

Thorndike [292] gave an intelligence examination to 8,564 pupils at the beginning of one school year and recorded the subjects which each pupil studied during the year. At the end of the year the pupils were retested, and the gains made in the test were put into relation with the subjects studied. Thorndike found that "studies taken make little or no difference upon gain made during the year in power to think" (at least insofar as abilities to deal with the words, numbers, and space forms on the intelligence test measure power to think). Both Thorndike and Hill find no support "for the general contention that reasoning can be trained in degrees at all commensurate with popular opinion."

White [319] worked with an experimental and control group, each having a mean age of almost thirteen years and equated for intelligence quotient. The experimental class was given an hour's teaching in logic each week for a period of three months. The lessons in logic were concerned with classification, inference, and emotional (or affective) thinking. At the end of three months each class was given a reasoning test, Ballard's English Construction Test, and a composition to write. White reports that there was a significant difference in favor of the experimental group on all three tests, and concludes: "From these results we may infer that lessons in logic do effect an improvement in habits of thought in school children."

Salisbury [256] set up her study to try to answer the following questions: What effect does training in logical organization (thought analysis and synthesis) as practiced through the medium of outlines and summaries have upon high school pupils as measured by changes in (1) intelligence scores, (2) mental age, (3) reading comprehension, (4) reading rate, (5) reasoning, and (6) performance in some similar study situation where transfer might be expected to occur? Is such training most effective in the seventh, ninth, or twelfth grade? Does such training operate better when conducted intensively (daily for six weeks) or when scattered intermittently through a semester, with lessons only two times a week?

The experiment was conducted in English classes of four midwestern high schools and included 474 students. Two of the four experiments were conducted at the ninth grade level, one at the seventh, and one at the twelfth. Pupils were equated for the experimental and control groups on the basis of intelligence quotient, reading ability, and mental age. The following are among the results reported.

1. Training in the conscious use of outlining as a method of study (as a learning skill) when taught through practice with general materials will transfer to specific study situations and tend to improve mastery on content subjects. (Gains in content subjects, as measured by achievement tests, were greater for experimental than for control groups.)

2. The mental skills involved in outlining and summarizing, described herein as the processes of logical organization, transfer to produce improvement in general thinking or reasoning ability, as tested by problems not related to the specific school curriculum.

3. Training in logical organization of the sort given in this investigation produces marked improvement in reading ability, slowing down somewhat the speed of reading typical study materials and greatly increasing comprehension.

4. Such training, given as early as the seventh grade, produces satisfying improvement in reading and reasoning, and especially in mastery of content subjects.

5. Such training produces highly significant improvement in reading, and mastery of content subjects when given either to ninth or twelfth grade pupils.

6. The effect of the training on I. Q. is not great, such gains as did occur probably being due to improved reading ability.

7. Training in logical organization appears to be somewhat more successful if given intensively during a short period of time than if given intermittently during a longer period.

8. Skill in outlining, as a study habit, is a highly successful aid to learning.

9. Improvement in thinking, as exemplified in reading comprehension, reasoning, and understanding of comprehensive units of content-subject materials, can be achieved in the public schools under normal classroom conditions by giving pupils directed practice in outlining and summarizing.

10. The training showed greatest effects upon pupil ability to earn scores on the reading test (Haggerty Reading Examination, Sigma 3). These wholly significant gains in reading ability for all four experiments

were accompanied by a slowing down in the rate of reading typical text-book materials, the experimental pupils taking from 1.5 to 2.5 minutes longer to read a standard selection at the end of the experiment than their matched controls, among seventeen matched pairs.[27]

In order to test the effectiveness of the teaching of critical thinking in the elementary schools Wrightstone [336] constructed a battery of tests designed to measure ability to (1) obtain facts, (2) interpret or explain the facts obtained, and (3) apply the conclusions or generalized facts to new or special situations. The tests were administered to pupils in the fourth, fifth, and sixth grades of the activity and the non-activity schools in New York City. The pupils in the experimental schools gained more than the pupils in the conventional schools. Wrightstone concludes:

. . . schools which profess critical thinking as a major objective and provide for its practice can improve the quality of pupil thinking. Under present practices the schools in this study which employ units of work and allow pupil participation in the planning of the units of work have shown that the pupils' powers in obtaining reliable facts, interpreting facts, and applying generalizations may be influenced perceptibly and significantly, even in the period of a year. With systematic instruction over a longer period of years it may be reasonably assumed that pupils who have the advantages of instruction which emphasize the defined aspects of critical thinking will have a definite superiority in terms of pupil growth and performance over pupils taught by conventional practices.[28]

Teller [288] set up an experimental and control group of students enrolled in the basic course in the history of education. Both groups attended classes five periods a week but in the experimental group one period was devoted specifically to group thinking in the interpretation of historical data. Teller reports that the experimental group showed greater improvement in ability to interpret data, and also developed a more critical attitude toward current educational problems.

[27] R. Salisbury. "A Study of the Transfer Effects of Training in Logical Organization." *Journal of Educational Research,* Vol. 28, No. 4, pp. 241–254, 1934.

[28] J. W. Wrightstone. *Appraisal of Newer Elementary School Practices,* pp. 194–195. Bureau of Publications, Teachers College, Columbia University, 1938.

Lewis [168] afforded students in his social studies course the opportunity to evaluate propaganda in learning situations through setting up an experimental unit in propaganda analysis. Scientific attitude and the ability to make distinctions between evidence and propaganda and between propaganda and authority were included in his goals of instruction. In evaluating the results of this special unit, Lewis concludes:

In this unified learning experience which involved social studies, science, mathematics, and English, the indication is that these students gained a functional understanding of the nature of propaganda and the techniques for evaluating it.

Schools may do much in aiding students to detect betrayal of fact and to adjust intelligently to realities of life. The transfer of these skills and techniques to life situations which involve making decisions and drawing conclusions warrants giving continued and increased emphasis to such training.[29]

Jewett [147] attempted to discover whether high school juniors and seniors could be taught through classroom instruction to detect and analyze propaganda. He reports:

The students who were taught under the experimental conditions showed a highly significant superiority over those in the control groups in ability to detect and analyze propaganda and to discriminate among articles containing different amounts of propaganda. Also the (experimental) students proved to be more cautious about making generalizations on the basis of insufficient data, according to the (Watson-Glaser) Generalization Test.

. . . A highly significant amount of growth was made on the (Watson-Glaser) Inference Test by the experimental class which contained students with a mean intelligence quotient of 118 and which was taught by the writer. A smaller amount of growth was made by the experimental classes in the three other schools.[30]

Biddle [21] worked with experimental and control students in five high schools and one college, using nine prepared lessons entitled "Manipulating the Public." His purpose was to make

[29] R. S. Lewis. "Building Pupils' Defenses Through a Unit on Propaganda." *Clearing House,* Vol. 13, No. 1, pp. 22–24, 1938.
[30] A. Jewett. "Detecting and Analyzing Propaganda." *English Journal,* pp. 105–115, February, 1940.

the students critical of emotional thinking, of propaganda devices commonly used, and of the point of view of the lessons themselves. Gullibility was measured by scoring the responses of students to a series of articles in a test given before and after the teaching of the nine lessons. In every school, the experimental group improved more than the control group.[31] About 42 per cent of the experimental group showed an outstanding improvement. Thirty-one per cent showed an improvement in critical attitude toward either nationalist or internationalist material alone. The author concludes:

> Improvement for a majority of students is based upon conscious transfer of the teaching. Other students it is difficult to account for. There may be differences among students in ability to change opinions on the basis of rational, intelligent persuasion. This needs investigation. On the whole, the material has proved its power to increase skepticism in response to literary material. This is an important result for democratic countries.

Osborne [222] reports a study set up to determine: (1) the effectiveness of a unit of instruction designed for use in teaching high school social studies pupils to resist propaganda, (2) the degree to which knowledge concerning a selected controversial social issue is associated with attitudes toward that issue and also with shift in attitude toward that issue stimu-

---

[31] In a careful and comprehensive analysis, Osborne [222] has shown that Biddle's test of ability to recognize tricks of propaganda "favored the experimentals in that it, like the lessons, dealt with international relations. The controls had no instruction in the forms in which propaganda concerning international relations commonly appear. Since both groups took the test before the period of instruction, it would appear difficult to contradict the contention that the experimentals might well be led to see a connection between the test and the teaching, and thus have an unfair advantage over the controls."

Osborne has further shown that Biddle used an incorrect formula to compute the standard error of the gains between the experimental and control groups and that the critical ratio of difference in gains was really only 1.56 instead of 17.55 as reported by Biddle. With reference to this point, Osborne concludes that "it is safe to say that the validity of Biddle's conclusions, as to the effectiveness of his instructional materials in reducing gullibility with respect to nationalist propaganda, can be questioned."

Biddle's use of an incorrect formula to compute the standard error of difference between two proportions likewise invalidates his conclusion that, with respect to intelligence, the difference between improvers and non-improvers is statistically significant since the difference is three times the standard error.

lated by reading a selection designed to shift that attitude, and (3) the degree to which intelligence is associated with attitudes toward the selected controversial social issue and also with shift of attitude toward that issue stimulated as described above.

In connection with deciding upon the method to use in order to develop pupil ability to resist propaganda, Osborne writes:

> Opinions vary as to the most effective method of education against propaganda. Two general methods have been suggested. The first method of teaching critical thinking is based on the conviction that there are no short-cuts whereby an individual can develop resistance to propaganda. According to this method, resistance to propaganda would be achieved through developing in the individual, throughout his school experience, habits of approaching conflict situations from an intellectual, problem-solving point of view. Content would be emphasized.
>
> The second method of teaching resistance to propaganda would make a direct study of the tricks or techniques of propaganda, and of how they appeal to our emotions and lead us to uncritical acceptance of opinions or suggested actions. Here the emphasis would be on "form" instead of "content." A considerable body of curricular literature is available suggesting student activities whereby this second method can be put into operation. Because of the recent popularization of this method in our schools, it was used in this study.[32]

Osborne used twenty pairs of eleventh and twelfth grade social studies classes, with one teacher for each pair, in seventeen Iowa high schools. By means of chance, one class in each pair was designated as an experimental class and the other as a control class. The pupils in each of the twenty experimental classes studied for six days a unit of instruction entitled "Public Opinion and Propaganda." During this six-day period, the pupils in each of the twenty control classes carried on their regular class work, and were assigned no work on the subject of propaganda.

Three weeks after the end of the instructional period, all pupils in both experimental and control groups were tested for attitudes and knowledge concerning capital punishment. Immediately thereafter all the students were given a propa-

[32] W. W. Osborne. "Teaching Resistance to Propaganda." *Journal of Experimental Education,* Vol. 8, pp. 1–17, 1939.

ganda reading selection, "Why Capital Punishment Is Necessary," following which, at the same sitting, the students were given a post-measurement of attitude toward capital punishment. Two weeks later all students were given a delayed measurement of attitude toward capital punishment. Some of Osborne's findings are given below.

Conclusions:

1. Even though there was strong evidence to indicate that the pupils in the experimental group did develop an increased awareness of the methods of the propagandist, the objective standard of effectiveness used in this experiment showed that the study of the unit of instruction, "Public Opinion and Propaganda," did not prove to be effective in developing resistance to propaganda on the part of these pupils.

2. Certain teachers reported that their experience with the unit had led them to doubt whether pupils could detect propaganda devices unless they had a background of information concerning the problem at issue.

3. The negligible correlations between measures of knowledge concerning propaganda devices and measures of immediate and delayed shift of attitude in response to propaganda as found in this study, strongly suggest that attempts to teach resistance to propaganda with respect to social issues by emphasis only on the "form" in which propaganda commonly appears will be unlikely to succeed. It seems *unlikely,* therefore, that even a longer time allotment for the unit of instruction used in this experiment would have developed greater resistance to propaganda on the part of the experimental group than on the part of the control group.

4. To the extent that pupils' reactions toward propaganda with respect to capital punishment, as found in this study, can be accepted as a basis for generalization, attitudes of senior high school social studies pupils toward social issues can be shifted in a predetermined direction by means of propaganda in the form of a literary selection even when careful study of methods of resisting propaganda has been completed by these pupils less than one month prior to their being subjected to such propaganda. In the absence of additional propaganda with the same or a counter emphasis, such shift of attitude tends to be relatively permanent as shown by the fact that, in this study, the shift was still statistically significant after a delay of two weeks.

5. The relation of knowledge and intelligence to attitude and attitude shift was found to be negligible in magnitude.

Educational Implications:

1. Even though a study of the "tricks" of propaganda does not alone appear to be an effective way of developing resistance to propaganda, the

strong motivating character of such study, as demonstrated in this experiment, should be utilized in other units designed for use in teaching resistance to propaganda. Additional experimentation should be carried on to determine the effectiveness of units of instruction which provide for the development of resistance to propaganda through attention to both the "form" and "content" in which propaganda commonly appears.*

2. Since the evidence presented by this study indicates that neither achievement nor intelligence, as commonly measured, is a dependable index of ability to resist propaganda, the writer suggests that experimentation be carried on to evaluate the effectiveness of units of instruction designed for use in developing the spirit of criticism with respect to social issues contemporaneously with the original study of such issues.

3. While the possession of knowledge and intelligence is no doubt necessary in order to do critical thinking, the results of this experiment strongly suggest that an individual may, according to commonly obtained measures, possess both these traits to a high degree and yet be highly susceptible to propaganda influences. Possibly critical thinking can be developed best when pupils are taught in such a manner, throughout their school experiences, that they must constantly use information in problem-solving situations and in such a manner that they are constantly forced to make tentative conclusions as a result. In other words, it is just possible that the way to teach critical thinking is to give pupils long-term practice in it.[33]

Judd [149] presents evidence indicating that our secondary and higher education has, by and large, emphasized the acquisition of information and recall, and has not specifically tried to develop ability to draw inferences from new data. Where higher mental processes (those in which the individual makes a large contribution through his own conscious effort) have been cultivated, an improvement in general ability to think critically is more likely to result. Judd writes:

There are many levels of intelligence and of intellectual achievement. There is no reason for distinguishing merely two levels, a very low and a very high. There is an uninterrupted series of steps leading up from the experiences which are externally conditioned, simple, and immature to the experiences which are higher because they emphasize systematically relations, abstractions, and broad generalizations. It is to the

---

* The author's study reported in this volume represents just the kind of experiment Osborne urges. However, this study was conceived and completed before Osborne's study was published.

[33] *Ibid.*

advantage of society that all individuals be stimulated to climb these steps as rapidly and as far as possible. The acceptance of this view means that the major task of the schools is to attempt to teach all individuals to make comparisons and draw contrasts, to look for explanations which will bring together ideas, to apply the systematic modes of thinking which the race has evolved, and to express clearly in language the relations between events and between facts. The schools have not adequately performed this task. Indeed, they have often directed pupils away from the path of real intellectual achievement by rushing over great collections of particular items of information and thus failing to stimulate the contemplative evaluation of items systematically arranged.[34]

Symonds [286], in his book *Education and the Psychology of Thinking,* based on an analysis of thought processes involved in problem-solving, observes that:

Thinking has general features in the matter of method but it also has specific features in subject matter. . . . In order to learn to think one must practice thinking in the situation in which it is to be used and on material on which it is to be exercised. This prevents the preparation of exercises to develop thinking in the abstract which will provide power to think effectively in situations in general. Certain of the early experiences which lead to discriminations and fundamental relationships are very nearly general. Certain skills, such as those used in reading and study, have wide application, but even these have their specific quality. For instance, it is much easier to read a book on economics if one has already done considerable reading in economics. . . . Thinking is not the application of independent units, one at a time, but rather a skillfully conducted interplay of habits and skills. . . . For this reason thinking cannot be trained *entirely* by analytical practice on vocabulary, outlining, reading, inference, etc. Acquiring skill in these separate elements contributes to the whole, but once acquired these separate skills cannot be immediately pieced together to form an integrated whole. The baseball player may employ batting practice, fielding practice, and pitching practice, but none of these suffices to give competence in meeting the various exigencies of the actual game. In short, practice in thinking itself is necessary for the improvement of thinking. There is no substitute for the actual wrestling with real problems in the development of thinking.[35]

[34] C. H. Judd. *Education as the Cultivation of the Higher Mental Processes,* p. 193. By permission of The Macmillan Company, publishers, New York, 1936.

[35] Percival M. Symonds. *Education and the Psychology of Thinking,* p. 235. By permission of the publishers, McGraw-Hill Book Company, New York, 1936.

Some very interesting data concerning the effectiveness of several different types of instructional devices in problem-solving are offered by Laycock [166]. Laycock presented three test problems to children of eleven and twelve years of age. His first test problem is based on the story of Cyrus' attack on the city of Babylon. The solution is for the attackers to divert the water from the Euphrates River, which ran under the city's walls, so that the attackers could then enter the city through the dry river bed.

The number of correct solutions given by the children after the first presentation was recorded. The children were then divided into five groups consisting of one control group (Group I) and four instructional groups. Each of the instructional groups was trained by a different method. All groups were then retested with the original problems.

Group II was given four training stories where "diverting" would solve the problem, but where the principle of diverting was not expressed in words and not related to the test problems.

In Group III the procedure was the same as for Group II, except that at the end of each training story the principle of diverting was expressed in language.

The procedure with Group IV was the same as for Group II, except that before the training stories were read the children were given a slip of paper stating that "The following stories may help you find out how Cyrus captured Babylon. You will be given another chance at the end to say how you think Cyrus did actually capture the city."

For Group V the procedure was the same as for Group III, i. e., the principle was formulated at the end of each story; in addition they were given the slip of paper as in Group IV.

The second problem, similar in type to the first, was the "Burglar Test," the solution for which was to be found in diverting the attention of the burglar. The third problem involved the understanding of a mechanical model, accompanied by an actual demonstration of the working of the model for Groups III and V.

All the groups showed a gain in the number of correct solutions when the problems were presented for the second time. With all three problems, however, Group V, which had the advantage of both the slip of paper and the statement of the guiding principle (or demonstration of the model) gained the most. With the Cyrus and Burglar "story" tests there was a progressive increase in gains from Group I to Group V, while in the mechanical models test, Group III, which was also shown a demonstration of the model, gained more than Group IV.

According to Laycock's study the most effective instructional method for helping pupils to understand a fundamental relation and learn to apply that understanding to the solution of other problems in which the same fundamental relation is involved consists of furnishing (1) an active direction to mental activity, (2) appropriate experience (as in the training material), and (3) means of attaining during the course of the experience a clear understanding of the guiding principles involved and their application to a variety of problems to which the same principles apply.

Waters [313] was concerned with a thought problem which took the form of a game between the subject and experimenter. The solution to the problem could be found if one perceived a certain arithmetical relationship or formula. The subjects were divided into six groups, each receiving a different method of instruction. In general, Waters' findings are in agreement with those of Laycock. The method which directed the subjects' attention to a significant aspect of the problem proved to be decidedly beneficial in learning. Some of Waters' instructional methods were detrimental, however, and others were of advantage only in helping the subjects to solve the first problem, but were of no help when the subject attacked a new problem on his own initiative.

Investigating whether concepts were better formed by beginning with the generalization or beginning with individual cases Fowler [100] found that beginning with the generalization and proceeding to individual cases is more effective provided the generalization is combined with an explanation which is understood by the pupils.

Apropos of training the dull child, Commins [68] observes that "Breaking up a thought problem into convenient steps and confining these to a few well-chosen fundamentals will help the dull child very much. His difficulty with generalization may be partly compensated for by multiplying the number of examples to which the principle applies."

Summary of Studies Concerning Training to Think Critically and Transfer of Training to Think Critically

The studies by Curtis, Caldwell and Lundeen, Downing, Noll, Peterson, Powers, Sinclair and Tolman, and Zepf in the field of science training; by Daily, Fawcett, Hall, Lazar, Parker, Perry, and Shendarker in the field of mathematics, and by Barlow, Biddle, Hill, Jewett, Jones, Salisbury, Teller, White, and Wrightstone in the fields of English, logic, and the social studies, all point to the conclusion that the content alone of any subject is not likely to give general training to the mind, and is not likely to develop a generalized ability to think critically.

A student does not tend to develop a general disposition to consider thoughtfully the subjects and problems that come within the range of his experience, nor is he likely to acquire knowledge of the methods of logical inquiry and reasoning and skill in applying these methods, simply as a result of his having studied this subject or that. There is no evidence that students acquire skill in critical thinking as a necessary by-product of the study of any given subject. On the other hand, almost any subject or project can be so taught as to put pupils on guard against hasty generalization, contradictory assertions, and the uncritical acceptance of authority. Thus, transfer of training from the study of logical reasoning and methods of evaluating the adequacy of evidence in a subject-matter field such as geometry or general science *can be brought about,* but it does not occur automatically.

In general the research indicates that if the objective is to develop in pupils an attitude of "reasonableness" and regard for the weight of evidence and to develop ability to think critically about controversial problems, then the component attitudes and abilities involved in thinking critically about such problems must be set up as definite goals of instruction. Specific training for the given objectives should be provided, and the processes and principles of reasoning which are involved must be made clear and usable to the students. This can be accomplished by guiding students to think through problems and to evaluate arguments concerned with precisely the kinds of issues in connection with which it is most desired to develop ability to think critically. The problems considered should be on the students' level of interest and maturity.

Training in abstracting, analyzing, outlining, summarizing, and generalizing have been found effective for improving both reasoning and reading ability (Barlow, Salisbury).

One's ability to apply knowledge to the solution of given problems is not in direct proportion to one's knowledge of facts in the field pertaining to those problems. Knowledge may sometimes be a result of superficial reading or rote memory; some persons with a good deal of factual knowledge in a field do not feel a sufficient stimulus for thought and thus do not undertake directive thinking and some persons are able to apply effectively a relatively limited knowledge of facts. In general, however, persons tend to make the fewest errors in judgment and reasoning in the situations in which they have had the most experience and concerning which they do know the pertinent facts (E. B. Moore).

The point of view of Wood and Beers that "thinking and thinking ability are certainly much less [than information and knowledge], if at all, under the control of teaching" is supported by the evidence of experimental studies (Hill, Salisbury, Thorndike) only when reasoning and thinking ability are considered as very largely synonymous with general mental ability or general intelligence. Hill, for example, reports that she found improvement in ability to deal with each of her four sets of reasoning material after training in that kind of material, and that the training was transferable in cases where the method of attack facilitated handling of the new type of material. Although Salisbury notes that the effect of her training in outlining and summarizing upon I. Q. is not great, she nevertheless reports "significant improvement in reasoning and reading ability."

There is no contradiction among the various findings when we recognize that general intelligence constitutes *a* part, but not the *only* part of what we mean by "reasoning ability" and "ability to think critically." The findings are then in agreement that on the one hand scores on general intelligence tests generally are not susceptible to appreciable improvement upon training, but that on the other hand attitudes of open-mindedness, intellectual responsibility, and a *desire* to have evidence for one's beliefs, as well as knowledge of the principles of logical reasoning and specific skills in applying those principles, are susceptible to appreciable improvement.

The efficacy of given training to improve ability to think critically and the amount and quality of transfer which occurs will be greatly influenced by: (1) the method of presentation, (2) the degree to which self-activity and personal experience are induced, (3) the means of furnishing precision, definiteness, and stability to the course of this activity, (4) the extent to which the desired outcomes are set up as definite goals of instruction, (5) the extent to which the processes of reasoning and guiding principles are made clear to the students, and (6) the degree of relationship or similarity between specific elements in the training and their existence in the new situations to which transfer is desired.

An individual's personality traits and attitudes affect his ability to think. Proper training will include the cultivation of a conscious attitude of readiness to consider in a thoughtful way the problems and subjects that come within the range of one's experience, as well as knowledge of the principles of logical reasoning together with some skill in applying those principles. Emphasizing both the attitudes and skills involved in critical thinking, Dewey [79] says:

Ability to train thought is not achieved merely by knowledge of the best forms of thought. . . . Moreover, there are no sets of exercises in correct thinking whose repeated performance will cause one to be a good thinker. The information and the exercises are both of value. But no individual realizes their value except as he is personally animated by certain dominant attitudes in his own character. . . .

If we were compelled to make a choice between these personal attitudes (open-mindedness, whole hearted interest, responsibility in facing consequences) and knowledge about the principles of logical reasoning . . . we should decide for the former. Fortunately, no such choice has to be made because there is no opposition between personal attitudes and logical processes. . . . What is needed is to weave them into unity.[36]

A study of the "tricks" of propaganda, or of propaganda devices, does not alone appear to be an effective way of developing resistance to propaganda (Osborne). Resistance to propaganda is likely to be achieved by developing in the individual throughout his school experience habits of approaching conflict situations from a problem-solving point of view and knowledge of and skill in methods of logical inquiry.

An individual's problem-solving ability is not increased for future occasions by providing him with ready-made rules and generalizations (Laycock, Waters). Verbal formulation should proceed from the student himself, wherever possible, and the instructor should serve only to give it greater accuracy, definition, and clearness (Commins, Fawcett, Laycock).

It is important to get *each* student to make his own verbal formulations and generalizations, to get each student to see and be able to apply the proper guiding principles, and not to assume that because one or a few especially bright students can make adequate verbal formulations the class as a whole thereby understands the points and principles involved.

For the dull child it will be helpful to break up a thought problem into convenient steps, each step dealing with a relatively easy principle. Each principle, in turn, needs to be illustrated in a number of examples to which it applies, and furthermore the child should be encouraged to suggest his own examples.

[36] *Op. cit.*, pp. 29, 34.

THE MEASUREMENT OF ABILITY TO THINK CRITICALLY

Several of the component abilities included under the concept of "ability to think critically" (as that phrase is used in the present study) are to some extent measured by tests of "general intelligence." It is beyond the scope of this study to describe intelligence tests. Consequently only instruments which have been developed to measure aspects of ability to think critically as distinct from "general intelligence" per se will be described.

One of the earliest tests of reasoning was Burt's Graded Reasoning Test. The type of problems presented in the test may be seen from the following illustration at the seven-year level:

I have bought the following Christmas presents: a pipe, a blouse, some music, a box of cigarettes, a bracelet, a toy engine, a bat, a book, a doll, a walking stick, and an umbrella. My brother is 18: he does not smoke, or play cricket, or play the piano. I want to give the walking stick to my father and the umbrella to my mother. Which of the above shall I give to my brother?

In 1925, Watson [314] published a test to measure prejudice defined as any tendency:

(Form A) to cross out, as distasteful, terms which represent one side or another of religious or economic controversies:

(Form B) to call sincere and competent persons who hold different opinions on religious and economic issues incompetent or insincere:

(Form C) to draw from given evidence conclusions which support one's bias but which are not justified by that evidence:

(Form D) to condemn in a group which is disliked activities which would be condoned or approved in some other group:

(Form E) to regard arguments, some of which are really strong and others of which are really weak, as all strong if they be in accord with the subject's biases, or all weak if they run counter to that bias: and

(Form F) to attribute to all people or objects in a group, characteristics which belong to only a portion of that group.

The Watson-Glaser Tests of Critical Thinking [315], developed in connection with this study, represent an experimental form of an effort to revise Watson's original tests of fair-mindedness. The revision eliminates problems concerning religious controversies, and measures aspects of critical thinking (such as recognition of unstated assumptions) which were not measured by Watson's original instrument. These tests are suitable for use in grades nine through college.

Zyve's [340] Stanford Scientific Aptitude Test, published in 1930, "is concerned with detecting a conglomerate of basic traits which enter into what may be called aptitude for science or engineering." Some of the exercises in this test measure abilities which are included under the concept of "critical thinking" as defined in this study. The exercises or sub-tests included in the Stanford Scientific Aptitude Test are called: (1) Experimental Bent, (2) Clarity of Definition, (3) Suspended Versus Snap Judgment, (4) Reasoning, (5) Inconsistencies, (6) Fallacies, (7) Induction, Deduction, and Generalization, (8) Caution and Thoroughness, (9) Discrimation of Values in Selecting and Arranging Experimental Data, (10) Accuracy of Interpretation, and (11) Accuracy of Observation. This test is suitable for use in grades eleven and twelve and for college students.

Hoff [129] developed a test consisting of 150 questions dealing with what he considered to be the five major components of scientific attitude, namely:

I. Conviction of universal basic cause-and-effect relations rendering untenable (a) superstitious beliefs in general, as "signs" or "good or bad luck," and charms; (b) "unexplained mysteries"; and (c) "beats all" attitude, commonly revealed by too ready credulity and tendency to magnify the importance of coincidence.

II. Sensitive curiosity concerning reasons for happenings coupled with ideals (a) of careful and accurate observation, or equally careful and accurate use of pertinent data previously collected by others; (b) of patient collecting of data; and (c) of persistence in search for adequate explanation.

III. Habit of delayed response, holding views tentatively for suitable reflection (varying with the matter in hand) to permit (a) adequate considerations of possible options, and (b) a continuous plan of attack, clearly looking forward to a prediction of the probable outcome or solution.

IV. Habit of weighing evidence with respect to its pertinence, soundness and adequacy.

V. Respect for another's point of view, an open-mindedness and willingness to be convinced by evidence.[37]

Below is an illustrative item from the test. The letters T–F–ID–DK beside the item represent the following answers: T, true; F, false; ID, insufficient data; DK, I do not know.

T–F–ID–DK   I always get exhausted more easily than the other boys in my gym class. My father says that I am all right, but the gym work is too difficult.

Hoff found correlations ranging from .14 to .39 among five classes of students who took both his test and the Stanford Scientific Aptitude Test.

Noll [218] constructed a test consisting chiefly of true-false items designed to measure each of the following six habits of thinking: accuracy, suspended judgment, open-mindedness, intellectual honesty, criticism (including self-criticism), and the habit of looking for true cause-and-effect relationships. This test is suitable for upper elementary and high school use.

Davis [78] developed two tests to measure scientific attitudes, a cause-and-effect relationship test and a fact-theory test. The test items are concerned with science information.

Downing [88] formulated a test to measure skill in the use of fifteen elements and safeguards involved in scientific thinking. The items are designed to test: (1) accuracy of observation, (2) ability to pick out pertinent elements from a complex situation, (3) ability to synthesize, (4) selective recall, (5) fertility of hypothesis, (6) ability clearly to define a problem before trying to solve it, (7) ability to hold in mind a complex of relations, (8) problem-solving ability, (9) judgment on adequacy of data, (10) tendency to try to solve a problem scientifically rather than just by trial and error, (11) tend-

[37] A. G. Hoff. "A Test for Scientific Attitude." University of Iowa Thesis, 1930.

ency to suspend judgment on moot questions, (12) ability to apply a rule or law, (13) tendency to test an hypothesis by collecting facts, (14) awareness of the danger of reasoning by analogy, and (15) ability to arrange data in sequence to make the conclusion evident. This test is suitable for use in grades eight through twelve, and with college freshmen.

Each of the above fifteen abilities or tendencies is measured by a single multiple-part question, which, from the point of view of sound test construction, raises serious questions concerning reliability and validity.

Hill [128] developed four reasoning tests: (1) Logic; (2) Problematic Arithmetic; (3) Generalization from Fables, and (4) Problematic Situations. Some of the items in her logic test were taken from Burt's [42] Absurdities Test. These tests are suitable for grades four through nine, and may be found in the Appendix to her monograph.

Wrightstone's [337] Test of Critical Thinking in the Social Studies contains three parts. Part I measures ability to obtain facts from data; Part II measures the ability to draw warranted conclusions from given facts; Part III measures the ability to apply general facts to explain other related facts or occurrences. This test is designed for use at the elementary level, but it may also be valuable at the high school level.

The Progressive Education Association, in its project called Evaluation in the Eight Year Study [240], under the direction of Ralph W. Tyler, developed a large number of tests designed to measure critical thinking with regard to specific fields, such as the reading of fiction, and applications of the principles of physics. Their tests which measure aspects of critical thinking as defined in this study, and which do not refer to a specific subject-matter field, are: Test 1.41—Social Problems; Test 2.51—Interpretation of Data; Test 5.11— Application of Certain Principles of Logical Reasoning; and Test 5.21—Nature of Proof. All these tests are suitable for grades nine through college.

Maller and Lundeen [188] have worked out a test to measure belief in superstitions.

Grim [113] developed interpretation-of-data tests from various kinds of social science facts and administered them, together with a standardized achievement test, to approximately thirty pupils in each of grades seven, eight, and nine. The coefficients of correlation between scores on the reading tests and scores on the interpretation-of-data tests are as follows: seventh grade, .66; eighth grade, .51; ninth grade, .52. Grim concludes: "It would seem that reading ability and ability to interpret data are somewhat related in the social studies, but not definitely enough to consider them as a single behavior."

Martin [191] devised a test of "critical reading," scores on which were found to correlate .77 with scores on the Watson-Glaser test battery.

Gans and Lorge [104] worked out a test of critical reading comprehension in the intermediate grades which requires the subject to select and reject reference material for use in solving given problems.

Other tests of critical thinking in special fields, such as Moore's [202] judgment test in science, are beyond the scope of this chapter.

Summary Concerning the Measurement of Ability to Think Critically

All the tests mentioned in this chapter might profitably be examined by anyone interested in the problem of the measurement of ability to think critically. Certain tests may be found much more suitable for given purposes than other tests; some tests, such as Wrightstone's, are suitable for use at the elementary level, while others are designed for the high school and college levels. The Wrightstone, Progressive Education Association, and Watson-Glaser tests are the most recent instruments specifically designed to measure aspects of ability to think critically.[38]

[38] Reviews of Wrightstone's test may be found in the 1940 Mental Measurements Yearbook. The Progressive Education Association and the Watson-Glaser Tests probably will be reviewed in the 1942 Yearbook. Oscar K. Buros (Editor). *The Nineteen Forty Mental Measurements Yearbook.* The Mental Measurements Yearbook, Highland Park, N. J., 1941.

In science the final arbiter is not the self-evidence of the initial statement, nor the façade of flawless logic which conceals it. A scientific law embodies a recipe for doing something, and its final validification rests in the domain of action.

—LANCELOT HOGBEN

CHAPTER III

A Description of Procedures: The Design of the Experiment

PRELIMINARY STEPS

AFTER the problems of the study were defined and delimited, the next step in procedure before the actual experiment could be undertaken was to prepare the materials to be used. This preparation included the construction of instruments to measure certain aspects of ability to think critically which were deemed important and subject to measurement by pencil-and-paper tests.[1] It also included writing the special lesson units which were to be used by the teachers of the experimental classes.

PUPILS AND CLASS ORGANIZATION

At the beginning of the second week in the fall semester of 1938, two seventh term (twelfth grade) English classes in each of two high schools (one school in New York City and the other in Newark, N. J.) were chosen as experimental groups. Each class was taught by a different teacher. These four experimental groups were matched with four control English classes in the same two schools.[2] Each control group was taught by a different teacher.[3] The factors for which the four groups were matched are indicated in Table 1. It may

[1] The construction of the critical thinking tests was done in collaboration with Professor Goodwin Watson, of Teachers College, Columbia University.

[2] One tenth grade experimental class and one tenth grade control class were selected for a subsidiary experiment. The experimental class was given a similar but modified form of special training. The results of this subsidiary experiment are reported following the report of the main experiment.

[3] Ten weeks were devoted to the experimental teaching period. The classes met for forty minutes a day, five days a week.

TABLE I

EXPERIMENTAL AND CONTROL GROUPS: FACTORS ON WHICH THEY WERE MATCHED

Group	Age			Av. School Grade Preceding Yr.			(Otis) I.Q.			Reading Score (Percentile Rank)		
	Mean	Range	S.D.*	Mean	Range	S.D.	Mean	Range	S.D.	Mean	Range	S.D.
E1 N = 25	16-1	14-9 to 17-7	.68	71.26	62.20 to 80.80	5.08	105.12	86 to 120	9.15	52.00	5-96	24.33
E2 N = 29	15-10	14-10 to 17-8	.64	75.32	61.5 to 89.74	7.69	107.03	92 to 123	8.57	47.00	8-88	22.89
E3 N = 32	16-8	15-1 to 18-3	.69	77.22	69.11 to 87.5	4.41	109.85	95 to 138	9.47	60.48	18-99+	22.66
E4 N = 41	17-1	15-11 to 18-8	.67	72.24	55.62 to 83.13	4.95	104.66	86 to 129	9.45	53.22	10-97	22.87
TOTAL E N = 127	16-6	14-9 to 18-8	.90	74.01	55.62 to 89.74	6.06	106.60	86 to 138	9.43	53.40	5-99+	23.56

C₁ N = 30	16-6	14-10 to 18-1	.84	73.20	60.51 to 91.80	9.06	104.17	83 to 128	11.18	53.03	7-99	28.41
C₂ N = 30	16-0	15-2 to 17-1	.58	77.67	60.90 to 93.12	6.81	109.20	87 to 135	15.20	68.53	20-99+	19.89
C₃ N = 37	16-7	14-5 to 17-11	.84	78.95	70.69 to 88.67	4.71	109.84	82 to 127	11.49	70.58	30-99	20.52
C₄ N = 35	16-10	15-1 to 18-6	.67	72.15	63.78 to 82.61	4.64	104.29	84 to 124	8.77	51.09	9-97	20.21
TOTAL C N = 132	16-6	14-5 to 18-6	.83	75.33	60.51 to 91.80	7.05	106.93	82 to 135	12.09	60.66	7-99+	24.06

Note: E = Experimental Group; C = Control Group; Means for *Total* E and *Total* C are composite means obtained by the formula

$$M = \frac{N_1 M_1 + N_2 M_2 + N_3 M_3 + N_4 M_4}{N}.$$

Composite standard deviations were obtained by the formula

$$\sigma_{com} = \sqrt{\frac{N_1\,(\sigma_1^2 + d_1^2) + N_2\,(\sigma_2^2 + d_2^2) + N_3\,(\sigma_3^2 + d_3^2) + N_4\,(\sigma_4^2 + d_4^2)}{N}}.$$

* These standard deviations are in years.

be noted that the composite mean percentile rank score for the twelfth grade on the Nelson-Denny Reading Test is seven points higher for the control group than for the experimental group.[4]

There was an almost even distribution of boys and girls both in the four experimental classes taken as one experimental group, and in the four control classes taken as one control group, as shown in Table 2.

TABLE 2

DISTRIBUTION OF BOYS AND GIRLS IN EXPERIMENTAL AND CONTROL GROUPS

Sex	Group				Total	Group				Total
	E_1	E_2	E_3	E_4	E	C_1	C_2	C_3	C_4	C
Girls	10	19	15	17	61	12	12	26	18	68
Boys	15	10	17	24	66	18	18	11	17	64

Both of the schools which cooperated in this experiment use a system of pupil grouping in each subject-matter class based on the grade received by the pupil in that subject at the end of the preceding semester. For example, students who received an English grade of 85 or better are grouped together and study an enriched English course; students who received a grade between 75 and 84 study the regular course; and students who received below 75 study a simplified course. All the experimental classes were in the middle group taking the regular English course. One of the control classes, C 2, was a superior group in English and was therefore taking an enriched course.

PARTICIPATING TEACHERS

The particular teachers invited to cooperate as teachers of the experimental classes were selected in each case upon recommendation of the head of the English department in

---

[4] Hereafter, the names "experimental group" and "control group" will refer respectively to the 127 cases in the four experimental classes and the 132 cases in the control classes. Individual classes will be referred to as E1, C1, etc.

that school as being persons who would probably be interested and who would cooperate fully with the experimenter. The teachers of the control groups were selected with three considerations in mind: (1) They were teaching the same grade English classes as the teachers of the experimental groups; (2) they were rated by their department head as being as competent in their professional field and in their teaching ability as the experimental teachers; and (3) they were rated by their department head as being approximately as popular with the students in that school as the teachers of the experimental classes.

THE TESTING PROCEDURE

After the experimental and control classes were chosen, the Gamma Test of the Otis Quick-Scoring Mental Ability Tests, Tests A, B–AR, C, D, E, and F of the Watson-Glaser Tests of Critical Thinking, and the Maller-Glaser Interest-Values Inventory were administered to all the students. When the testing was completed the teachers of the experimental classes took up the work outlined in the lesson units, while the teachers of the control classes took up the regular English work outlined in the course of study for the grade which they were teaching.

It so happened that in both New York and Newark the syllabus for the seventh term (twelfth grade) called for study of Macaulay's *Life of Johnson,* essays by Bacon, Morley, Addison, Steele, and Stevenson, a study of newspapers, and included among its objectives the development of ability to think critically. The teachers of both the experimental and control classes, then, were trying to develop in students the ability to think critically. The control teachers, using their own methods, taught the content outlined in the New York and Newark syllabi respectively. The experimental teachers used both their own methods and the procedures suggested in the lesson units. They supplemented the content outlined in the units by other materials which they selected as pertinent to the interests and needs of their students.

In December, 1938, the experimental and control classes were retested with the Otis and the Watson-Glaser tests, and in addition took the Nelson-Denny Reading Test and filled in the status sheet concerning the socio-economic background of the home.

TYPES OF DATA WITH WHICH THIS STUDY IS CONCERNED

This study is concerned mainly with four types of data.[5] One type of primary importance consists of the material suggesting and illustrating methods, processes, and learning situations by means of which pupils are likely to acquire an attitude of regard for the weight of evidence, and gain understanding of the methods of logical inquiry and reasoning, together with some skill in applying those methods. The second type of data consists of the content material to which, in this study, the methods and processes were applied.[6] The third type of data consists of various kinds of measures, in the form of test scores obtained from the students in both the experimental and control groups. Some of these measures were made at the beginning and at the end of the period of experimental teaching. Others, which were not considered likely to be affected by the special instruction given to the pupils in the experimental classes, such as a rating of the socio-economic level of the home, were made only once. The fourth type of data consists of written expressions of opinion by students at the close of the experiment describing the attitudes, habits, and abilities (if any) thought to have been derived from the special work in critical thinking, and stating the aspects of the work liked most and least. These data also include the judgments and impressions of the teachers of the experimental classes regarding the values and shortcomings of the specially developed lesson units as aids to

[5] Data are defined as material serving as a basis for discussion and inference; material furnished for study.
[6] The first and second types of data will be found in the Lesson Units described in this chapter.

developing in students some of the component attitudes and abilities involved in critical thinking.

INSTRUMENTS AND MATERIALS EMPLOYED
TESTS

1. *The Watson-Glaser Tests of Critical Thinking.*[7] These tests are designed to provide problems and situations which require the application of some of the important abilities involved in critical thinking. They represent an extensive revision of the Watson tests of fair-mindedness, published in 1925.[8] An explanation of the nature and purpose, and the validity and reliability of each of the tests employed follows.[9] A portion of each test is reproduced in the Appendix.

a. Tests A1 and A2: A Survey of Opinions. Tests A1 and A2 are two parts of a single instrument designed primarily to show the extent to which a person tends to be consistent in the beliefs he holds with reference to certain current social issues. Each statement in Test A1 is paralleled by its opposite in Test A2, and the two are so incompatible that a critical thinker who agreed with one could not very well accept the other. For example, the first question in Test A1 reads: "In general the wages or salaries persons receive are a fair measure of the value to society of the service they render." The paired opposite in Test A2 reads: "In general, the wages or salaries persons receive are not a fair measure of the value to society of the service they render."

In addition, Tests A1 and A2 yield two other scores which may be of some interest or diagnostic value, although they are not so clearly measures of critical thinking.

The "P score" shows agreement with what the authors of the tests conceive to be a progressive position, supporting

---

[7] Goodwin Watson and E. M. Glaser. *The Watson-Glaser Tests of Critical Thinking.* World Book Company, Yonkers-on-Hudson, 1941. In press. The experimental edition of the tests which was the edition used in this study, was published by the Institute for Propaganda Analysis, New York, 1938.

[8] Goodwin Watson. *The Measurement of Fair-mindedness,* 1925.

[9] The reliability coefficients reported are based on the earlier form of the tests of critical thinking, which have since been revised. The revised battery contains tests which were not among those in the earlier battery.

political and economic democracy, civil liberties, the welfare of all the people, and equality of opportunity. Because statements are paired, half assert the progressive view and half the more reactionary, suppressive, and intolerant attitude. These terms carry emotional connotations, and the authors recognize that although they have attempted to define a position held by liberals and progressives, there may be some who think of themselves as progressives or liberals who would disagree with the key at some points. Criterion groups, selected during test construction, confirm the interpretations of the authors, but there is no absolute standard of liberalism or progressivism.

The third score, or "U score," is obtained simply by counting the number of statements on Tests A1 and A2 which are answered "Undecided." A low U score indicates a readiness to take a positive stand on various controversial questions; a high U score may arise from ignorance, or pedantry, or resistance to the test, or neurotic inability to reach a decision, or from a justifiable feeling that the evidence does not warrant a definite opinion. The U score will be of interest chiefly as one behavior characteristic to be interpreted in each case in the light of more comprehensive knowledge of the whole individual personality.

Validity: The validity of Tests A1 and A2 is indicated by: (1) The fact that a jury of fifteen judges, selected for their special training in logic and language meaning, unanimously agreed that the paired opposite items in tests A1 and A2 do state views which, from the point of view of logical consistency, are mutually exclusive. (2) The fact that the P score distinguished clearly between two criterion groups known to differ in their views on socio-economic problems. One group was known to support the progressive and the other the reactionary position (as here conceived).

Reliability: The test-retest coefficient of reliability of total score for the two sections, based on 100 cases, was found to be .88; the correlation of scores on Section I with scores on Section II was found to be .85.

b. Test B–AR; General Logical Reasoning. The General Logical Reasoning Test measures ability to think in accord with the rules of logic, upon material that does not involve controversial social issues. Part One contains ten exercises of the syllogistic type; Part Two contains fifteen exercises presented in paragraph form with a more elaborate statement of evidence and situation. Not more than one of the proposed conclusions follows logically from the facts as stated in each exercise.

This test parallels very closely Test 3, the Applied Logical Reasoning Test, in which pupils are tested for their ability to do straight thinking about controversial social, economic, and political issues. Failure in Test 3 may be due to bias or to lack of ability in logic, or both. The General Logical Reasoning Test is intended to show whether or not the pupil is able to do logical thinking when the content is not weighted with strong feeling.

Validity: The test is designed to measure ability to perceive certain types of logical implications and think in accord with the rules of logic upon material that does not involve controversial social issues. It must do that with fidelity within the limitations of the pencil-and-paper test situations, because the logical implications are present in every problem. If the student sees them and thinks in accord with the rules of logic, presumably he will mark the correct responses, and thus obtain a high score; if he does not see them, and guesses, then he is likely to obtain a relatively low score. There is only one right answer to each question, and the key has been validated by unanimous agreement among a jury of fifteen persons selected for their training in logic.

Reliability: The test-retest coefficient of reliability, based on fifty cases (one week interval between test and retest), was found to be .82.

c. Test C: Inference Test. The Inference Test is designed to measure ability to judge the probable truth or falsity and the relevancy of inferences drawn from given statements of fact. The persons taking the test are directed to consider the data given in each statement as true, and then to judge whether the inference or conclusion drawn is *true, false, probably true, probably false,* or whether the inference is based upon evidence so insufficient that a judgment, to be accurate, must place it in a category labeled *insufficient data.*

The scoring has been arranged so that from the manner in which a student responds to the various items in the test, one may obtain a measure (within the limitations of paper-and-pencil responses) of (1) the student's general accuracy in judging the degree of truth or falsity of inferences or conclusions drawn from given facts; (2) the tendency to err in the direction of (*a*) uncritical acceptance of conclusions which are not supported by the evidence, or (*b*) failure to recognize a conclusion as probable or improbable when the evidence does not warrant such an inference; and (3) hypercritical rejection of conclusions which are supported by the evidence.

Validity: Each statement and each conclusion inferred from the statement, was submitted to a group of fifteen judges, trained in logic and scientific method. All the conclusions included in this test were unanimously agreed upon by the judges with respect to whether they were definitely true inferences from the data, probably true, false, or probably false, or whether it was impossible to determine their truth or falsity from the data given. The test has significantly distinguished between two groups of students previously identified by science teachers as appearing markedly able and markedly poor in ability to reason accurately and to think logically.

Reliability: The test-retest coefficient of reliability, based on fifty cases (one week interval between test and retest), was found to be .86.

d. Test D: Generalization Test. The Generalization Test contains a number of statements with the first word omitted. The student is to select one of the five words, ranging from "All" to "No," which would, in his opinion, most truly and accurately complete the statement. The purpose of the test is to discover the student's ability to generalize correctly, and particularly his ability to refrain from rash over-generalizations. If a student selects "All" or "No" as the word which most truly and accurately completes the sentence, he has gone beyond the available evidence, and has made a sweeping generalization for which there is no factual, objective basis.

An additional purpose of the test is to compare a student's ability to generalize on different types of material. The ten statements in Part I of the test are not concerned with controversial socio-economic or political issues, while all of the ten statements in Part II of the test involve such issues. This provides an opportunity to compare a subject's score on Part I with his score on Part II, and may indicate something about the operation of his biases.

Validity: A jury of fifteen persons selected for their training in scientific method and logic determined the key. Agreement was 100 per cent in most cases but on some items either of two responses will be given full credit. Partial credit is given, in the scoring key, for responses which, although not the best one, are still within the moderate categories.

Reliability: The test-retest coefficient of reliability, based on fifty cases (one week interval between test and retest), was found to be .88.

e. Test E: Discrimination of Arguments. Test E has been devised to measure ability to distinguish between strong, sound, relevant arguments and those that are weak, unsound, and irrelevant. On each of ten questions four arguments are presented; two are pro and two con; one on each side is strong and the other weak. It has been found that prejudiced persons tend to exaggerate the strength of arguments which support their positions and to belittle the opposing considerations. This test reveals the extent to which the subject can weigh arguments fairly, regardless of whether they uphold or attack his own position. The test further reveals in some subjects a tendency to be uncritical or hypercritical with reference to arguments. The issues are chosen from the area of socio-economic controversy.

Validity: Arguments were submitted to fifteen judges selected for their superior intelligence, training in thinking, and for fair-mindedness. They were revised until all judges agreed on the Strong or Weak Classification.

Reliability: The test-retest coefficient of reliability, based on 100 cases (one week interval between test and retest), was found to be .76.

f. Test F: Evaluation of Arguments.* This test endeavors to measure appreciation of four principles relating to proof in argument. The principles are: (1) If certain premises are accepted, then valid inferences which follow from those premises must also be accepted. (2) Crucial words or phrases must be precisely defined, and a changed definition will produce a changed conclusion although the argument from each definition is logical. (3) The validity of an *indirect* argument depends upon whether all the possibilities have been considered. (4) A logical argument cannot be disproved by ridiculing the arguer or his arguments, or by attacking his motives, etc. Each test item consists of a paragraph followed by three alternative conclusions, only one of which properly follows from the data given in the paragraph. Following the conclusions six "reasons" are listed, only one of which properly explains why the correct conclusion is logically correct.

Validity: The content validity of this test is, in a sense, automatically established. That is, according' to the rules of logical inference, there is only one right answer to each exercise. And among the six statements given with each exercise, from which the subject is to check one which supports his reasoning leading to the conclusion he has checked, only one is logically relevant in support of the correct conclusion. A subject who consistently selects the one valid conclusion and the one valid supporting statement is manifesting an aspect of logical sensitivity related to ability to draw correct inferences from arguments.

Reliability: The test-retest coefficient of reliability, based on fifty cases (one week interval between test and retest), was found to be .83.

---

* The situations used in this test are contained in a longer test developed by the P. E. A., Evaluation in the Eight Year Study, and have been adapted with permission from Dr. Ralph W. Tyler, director of the Evaluation Committee.

2. *The Otis Quick-Scoring Mental Ability Test.*[10] (Gamma Test, for High School and Colleges.) The purpose of the test is to measure mental ability—thinking power or the degree of maturity of the mind.

Reliability: The reliability, based on administration to 1,007 pupils, was found to be .86.

3. *The Nelson-Denny Reading Test.*[11] The test consists of two parts: (1) a test of vocabulary; and (2) a test of ability to read and understand paragraphs. There are 100 words in the vocabulary test, and nine selections of approximately 200 words each in the paragraph test.

Reliability: The reliability, as determined by finding the correlation between the two forms of test, is .91.

4. *The Maller-Glaser Interest-Values Inventory.*[12] This inventory is designed to measure the relative dominance of four major types of interest or basic values which are found within the individual: Theoretic, Aesthetic, Social, and Economic.

Validity: The test was given to four groups of persons (college students and adults) whose interests, as revealed in their studies and occupations, correspond to these four interest-values. Only those items were retained which significantly differentiated the four groups; that is, items wherein each of the four alternatives was selected most frequently or given the greater preference by the persons in the corresponding value-group. The coefficient of contingency between the scores and the independent classification into four groups is .84.

Reliability: The reliability of the test, as determined by the test-retest method, was found to be .816 (coefficient of contingency), and when corrected for coarse grouping was found to be .942 ± .008. The coefficients of reliability for the individual values were as follows:

[10] A. S. Otis. *Otis Quick-Scoring Mental Ability Tests.* 1937.
[11] M. J. Nelson and E. C. Denny. *The Nelson-Denny Reading Test.* 1929.
[12] J. B. Maller and E. M. Glaser. *The Interest-Values Inventory.* 1939.

	Theoretic	Aesthetic	Social	Economic
Test-retest after 10-day interval	.91	.93	.92	.87
Test-retest after 3-month interval	.71	.82	.70	.75

5. *Status Sheet.* The Status Sheet was devised by the author for use in this study for the purpose of obtaining information concerning the socio-economic background of the home. It is reproduced in the Appendix.

LESSON UNITS

There were eight lesson units in the original series developed for use by the teachers of the experimental classes. They were entitled: (1) Recognition of Need for Definition, (2) Logic and the Weight of Evidence, (3) The Nature of Probable Inference, (4) Deductive and Inductive Inference, (5) Logic and the Method of Science, and Some Characteristics of Scientific Attitude, (6) Prejudice as a Factor Making for "Crooked Thinking," (7) Values and Logic, and (8) Propaganda and "Crooked Thinking."

After the conclusion of the experiment, on the basis of the criticisms by the teachers and students who participated, criticisms from colleagues and professors at Teachers College, Columbia University, and on the basis of the author's recognition of certain weaknesses after observing the material used in the classroom, the units were extensively revised and reworked into five more comprehensive units entitled: (1) Language and Clear Thinking, (2) Generalization and Probable Inference, (3) Critical Thinking and Scientific Method, (4) Prejudice and Confused Thinking, and (5) Propaganda and Public Opinion.[13]

The first two of the original units are presented as samples of the kind of lesson outline with which the experimental

[13] These revised units are contained in the Appendix of the typewritten copy of this dissertation which is available in the Teachers College Library. A further revision of these units is now under way, and is expected to be published by the World Book Company in 1942 in the form of a textbook for students, with an accompanying teacher's guide. Five of the original units, in precisely the form in which they were given to the teachers of the experimental classes, are published in the *Group Leader's Guide to Propaganda Analysis,* by Violet Edwards, pages 221–240.

teachers actually worked. These units are much briefer than the revised units. Each of the original units deals with only a few main points. The limitation of the period of special instruction to ten weeks, during which there were several school holidays, necessitated a less comprehensive approach to the problems considered than is suggested in the revised units. The contents of the revised units, however, can of course be cut and adapted to meet time and other limitations in a given situation. It might be further noted that in the original units, the "Knowledge Objectives" were discussed only very briefly, whereas in the revised form they are developed more fully and other objectives have been added. The "Essential Readings for Teachers," however, are nearly the same in the earlier as in the revised units. There was thus greater need for the teachers of the experimental classes to do the background reading rather thoroughly than there would have been if they had been given the more comprehensive units.

Unit 1: Recognition of Need for Definition

I. OBJECTIVES

A. Knowledge Objectives

1. To know what is meant when one refers to "ambiguous words, phrases, slogans, or symbols," and to be able to recognize them.

2. To understand something of the operation of such propaganda devices as "name calling" and "glittering generalities."

     The application of a "bad name" to a person or group is designed to make us form a judgment to *reject and condemn,* without examining the evidence. The application of a "good name"—like "liberty," "social justice," "the right to work" —is a means by which the propagandist identifies his program with virtue by the use of "virtue words."

3. To know what we mean by "emotionally toned words" and to be able to recognize them in argumentation.

     For example: Those who show enthusiasm in support of proposals with which a speaker disagrees are "extremists"; while those showing similar enthusiasm on his own side are called "staunch."

4. To understand something of the purpose and nature of definition.

Logically, definitions aim to lay bare the principal features or structure, of a concept, partly in order to make it definite, to delimit it from other concepts, and partly in order to make possible a systematic exploration of the subject matter with which it deals—to state those features of a thing from which other features follow. For example, we define a triangle as "a plane figure, bounded by three straight lines, and having three angles." The component "plane figure" is called the *genus,* which tells us the kind or class of things which a triangle belongs to; the other component, "bounded by three straight lines and having three angles," is that part of the essence which distinguishes a triangle from other species in the same genus—for circles, ellipses, and so on are also "plane figures." This part of the definition is called the *differentia.*

5. To understand the rules for satisfactory definitions.
   a. A definition must give the essence of that which is to be defined.
   b. A definition must not be circular; it must not directly or indirectly contain the subject to be defined.
   c. A definition must be in positive rather than negative terms wherever possible.
   d. A definition should be expressed in clearly understood, literal language, and not in obscure or figurative language.

B. Appreciation Objectives
Students should recognize the necessity for clarity of definition in matters where precise thinking is essential, and should manifest this appreciation in classroom discussion, in their reading of newspapers, listening to speeches, etc.

II. BASIC CONCEPTS OR GENERALIZATIONS INVOLVED
It is necessary that crucial words and phrases be defined in argumentation, so that people can agree on the things to which these words refer, and thus minds can meet. Otherwise these words can carry very different meanings and different emotions to different people. Suppose that someone makes the following statement:
"Social justice and a good life for our people will only be achieved by courageous leadership in crushing our enemies." In order for this statement to have any meaning, we must agree on what is meant by "social justice" and a "good life"—recognize their distinguishing characteristics—then agree on what we mean by "courageous" leadership, and who our "enemies" are, and finally,

if we can agree on the latter, we must try to see how the crushing of these enemies will bring us what we have agreed to consider "social justice" and the "good life."

III. MATERIALS

A. Institute for Propaganda Analysis Monthly Bulletins, Nos. 2 and 3, Vol. I, 1938.

B. The books referred to in the bibliography suggested in this unit.

IV. PROCEDURE

Begin the work with a consideration of the importance of definition in matters which are claiming the interest of the pupils. Follow the method used by Fawcett (pp. 30–34). Put one of the paragraphs analyzed in Propaganda Analysis Bulletin No. 3 on the blackboard; ask students what it means, and ask further questions as indicated in the Bulletin. Follow suggestions in Chapter I in Thouless' book for calling attention to emotional meanings. See stenographic report of class in critical thinking.

V. LEADS INTO OTHER ACTIVITIES IN DAILY LIFE: HOMEWORK

Have someone read to the class current newspaper material where reference is made to "Reds," "un-American," "Reactionary," "Economic Royalist," etc., and have pupils stop reader when they feel the need for definition. Have them avoid quibbling, however. Each student should provide himself with an 8½″ x 11″ loose-leaf notebook. First homework assignment might be to have students clip an editorial from a newspaper or magazine, paste it on the first page of the notebook, and then underline in ink any examples of "glittering generalities," and in red pencil or crayon any examples of "name-calling." Papers, with name, date, and lesson number should be handed in by pupils at next meeting of class. Teacher should correct papers and return them to pupils for their notebooks.

VI. ESSENTIAL READINGS FOR TEACHERS

1. Fawcett, H. P. *The Nature of Proof*, pp. 10–12, 30–34, 46–52. Bureau of Publications, Teachers College, Columbia University, 1938.

2. Clarke, E. L. *The Art of Straight Thinking*, Chap. VI. D. Appleton-Century Co., New York, 1929.

3. Thouless, R. H. *How to Think Straight*, Chap. I. Simon and Schuster, New York, 1938.

4. Cohen, M. R. and Nagel, E. *An Introduction to Logic and Scientific Method*, pp. 224–241. Harcourt, Brace & Co., New York, 1934.

5. Institute for Propaganda Analysis Monthly Bulletins, Nos. 2 and 3, Vol. I, 1938.

Unit 2: Logic and the Weight of Evidence

I. OBJECTIVES

  A. Knowledge Objectives

    1. To understand the meaning of "logic," "evidence," "proposition," "implication," "relevant," "inference," "valid," "generalization," "presumption of fact."

    2. To understand the distinction between "inference" and "implication."

      For example: *Implication* is an objective relation or necessary connection existing between propositions. *Inference* refers to the psychological process of seeing and drawing or deducing the conclusion which is implied. An implication may hold even if we do not know how to infer one proposition from another.

    3. To understand what is meant by "conclusive evidence or proof."

    4. To understand something of the nature of logical implication.

      The specific task of logic is the study of the conditions under which one proposition necessarily follows and may therefore be deduced from one or more others, regardless of whether the latter are in fact true. Logical implication does not depend upon the truth of our premises. Whether a proposition is true or false, the test as to whether there is a logical implication between one proposition and another is the impossibility of the former being true and the latter being false.

    5. To understand what is meant by partial evidence or probable inference, and the difference between it and conclusive evidence.

      For example: Suppose we call a friend, and are informed that he is not at home, but went to visit his dentist. Suppose it is also definitely established that most persons visit a dentist because they want work done on their teeth. It would be probable inference, then, that our friend went there for professional services in connection with his teeth. But not necessarily; he might have gone to pay a bill, to try to sell something to the dentist, for a social call, or for any number of other reasons. But if we had established that ALL persons who visit dentists do so because they wish services in connection with their teeth, then it would necessarily follow that our friend had gone for that purpose.

6. To understand something of the use and application of logic.

Formal logic gives us the *necessary* conditions for valid inference and enables us to eliminate false reasoning, but that is not *sufficient* to establish any material or factual truth in any particular field. "Any competent electrician can adjust our electric lights, but we think it necessary that an engineer who has to deal with new and complicated problems of electricity should be trained in theoretical physics. A theoretical science is the basis of any rational technique. In this way logic, as a theoretical study of the kinds and limitations of different inferences, enables us to formulate and partially mechanize the processes employed in successful inquiry. Actual attainment of truth depends, of course, upon individual skill and habit, but a careful study of logical principles helps us to form and perfect techniques for procuring and weighing evidence."*

7. To understand what is meant by "thinking," following the explanation of Dewey, in Chapter I of his book, *How We Think*.

For example: The origin of thinking is some perplexity, some confusion or doubt. Given a difficulty, the next step is suggestion of some way out, the formation of some tentative plan or project, the consideration of some solution for the problem. The sources of the suggestion are past experience and a fund of relevant knowledge at one's command.

B. Appreciation Objectives

1. The recognition of the general need of evidence for what we or others believe or question; appreciation of the need for having ground for our opinions, and of asking for evidence before believing assertions from others on matters which are not well established.

2. Appreciation of the fact that in daily life we must frequently act and make judgments about matters where the evidence one way or another is far from conclusive, and that while we must often act quickly and decisively, we must hold our minds open to other evidence which may later turn up.

3. Respect for reason and truth as determined by the weight of evidence.

II. Basic Concepts or Generalizations Involved

A. Reflective thinking includes a conscious and voluntary effort to establish belief upon a firm basis of evidence and rationality.

*M. R. Cohen and E. Nagel *An Introduction to Logic and Scientific Method*, p. 23, 1934.

B. Logical implication does not depend upon the truth of our premises.

C. A proposition is not necessarily false, or proved to be so, if an argument in its favor is seen to rest on falsehood. A good cause may have bad reasons offered in its behalf.

D. The history of human error shows that a general consensus or widespread, unquestioned feeling of certainty does not preclude the possibility that the future may show us to be in error.

III. MATERIALS

A. Books listed in bibliography below.

B. Illustrative material to be found in newspapers—particularly in the school publication, if there is one, and bearing on problems in which students themselves have a real interest.

C. Material in Progressive Education Association Test 5.3, called "Critical Evaluation of Newspaper Articles and Editorials."

D. Distribute copy of "Interpretation of Data" test to each pupil at close of unit.

IV. PROCEDURE

Ask students for their ideas about meaning of the words to be defined. Do not spend too much time, however, on any one word. As soon as students begin to approximate a definition, summarize their thinking into more precise terms and write a satisfactory definition on the blackboard, asking students to copy into notebooks. (See definitions accompanying this unit.) In one or two cases, show how the definition you give conforms to the rules for satisfactory definition taken up in unit No. 1. After explaining difference between inference and implication, write a syllogism on the board, and ask for volunteers, or call on poorer students, to point out difference. Use illustration from Cohen and Nagel (pp. 6–7) about inhabitants in New York City and number of hairs on head of any one inhabitant, or some other example of your own to illustrate conclusive proof based on the acceptance of given premise, or given evidence. Then ask students to give examples. Follow Cohen and Nagel, and Dewey, for the balance of the knowledge objectives, using illustrative material of your own, and the first exercise in the Progressive Education Association Test 5.3 ("Critical Evaluation of Newspaper Articles and Editorials").

V. LEADS INTO OTHER ACTIVITIES IN DAILY LIFE: HOMEWORK

Ask students to list superstitions they hear commonly expressed and for which they believe there is no adequate evidence or ground for belief. Have students do (as homework) first two problems in the "Interpretation of Data" test.

VI. Essential Readings for Teachers
1. Cohen, M. R. and Nagel, E. *An Introduction to Logic and Scientific Method,* Chap. I. Harcourt, Brace, New York, 1934.
2. Dewey, John. *How We Think,* Chap. I. D. C. Heath & Co., New York, 1933.
3. Fawcett, H. P. *The Nature of Proof,* Appendix, Part I. Bureau of Publications, Teachers College, Columbia University, 1938.
4. Thouless, R. H. *How to Think Straight.* Simon & Schuster, New York, 1939.
5. Noll, Victor. "The Habit of Scientific Thinking." *Teachers College Record,* Vol. 35, pp. 1–9, 1933.

MATERIALS GIVEN TO TEACHERS OF EXPERIMENTAL CLASSES

In addition to the lesson units, each of the teachers of the experimental classes received a general introductory statement concerning the purpose of the experiment, a set of books (items 24–28 on the list below), copies of certain bulletins issued by the Institute for Propaganda Analysis, certain tests devised by Dr. Ralph Tyler and his associates in the Evaluation in the Eight Year Study of the Progressive Education Association, certain practice exercises and problems devised by the author, and two special manuscripts written by Professor Helen M. Walker of Teachers College, Columbia University, which she distributes to students in her course in Statistical Inference. Below is a complete list of the materials given to the teachers of the experimental classes.

1. Introduction to the Problem (An Experimental Study of the Development of Critical Thinking on Controversial Issues).
2. Unit 1: Recognition of Need for Definition.
3. Unit 2: Logic and the Weight of Evidence.
4. Unit 3: The Nature of Probable Inference.
5. Unit 4. Deductive and Inductive Inference.
6. Unit 5: Logic and the Methods of Science, and Some Characteristics of Scientific Attitude.
7. Unit 6: Prejudice as a Factor Making for "Crooked Thinking."
8. Unit 7: Values and Logic.
9. Unit 8: Propaganda and "Crooked Thinking."
10. Definitions of Logical Terms.

11. Stenographic Report of a Classroom Lesson in Critical Thinking (conducted by the author with a freshman class at New College, Columbia University).
12. "Critical Evaluation of Newspaper Articles and Editorials" (P.E.A. Test 5.3).
13. "The Nature of Proof" (P.E.A. Test 5.2-A).
14. "Sample and Universe" (adapted from an unpublished manuscript written by Professor Helen M. Walker, Teachers College, Columbia University).
15. "Probability and the Nature of Probable Inference" (same as 14 above).
16. Exercises in Probability (test—supplied to students, same as 14 above).
17. "Interpretation of Data" (P.E.A. Test 2.5—supplied to students).
18. A Problem in Scientific Thinking.
19. "Are You Learning to Weigh Evidence?" (test)
20. "Are You Learning to Form Reasoned Conclusions on Controversial Matters?" (test)
21. Institute for Propaganda Analysis Letter. November, 1937.
22. Institute for Propaganda Analysis Bulletin, *How to Detect Propaganda.* December, 1937.
23. Institute for Propaganda Analysis Bulletin, *Propaganda Techniques of German Fascism.* May, 1938.
24. *An Introduction to Logic and Scientific Method* by M. R. Cohen and E. Nagel.
25. *Straight and Crooked Thinking* (now called *How to Think Straight*) by Robert Thouless.
26. *The Nature of Proof* by Harold P. Fawcett.
27. *The Art of Straight Thinking* by E. L. Clarke.
28. "The Habit of Scientific Thinking" by Victor Noll.

Finally, the teachers of the experimental classes were given the following written directions for administering the tests and using the materials given to them.

To the Teachers of the Experimental Classes

A. Please study carefully the Manual of Directions to each of the following tests, before the time for administering them. Administer the tests approximately in the following order:

1. A Survey of Opinions Test (Test A1—Form 1)
2. Logical Reasoning Test (Test B1)
3. Inference Test (Test C1)

4. Generalization Test (Test D1).
5. Discrimination of Arguments Test (Test E1)
6. Evaluation of Arguments Test (Test F1)
7. Survey of Opinions Test (Test A1—Form 2)
8. Otis Quick-Scoring Test of Mental Ability (Gamma—Form A)
9. The Interest-Values Inventory.

B. It is not absolutely essential that the tests be given in the above order. The tests vary in the average length of time required to complete them; adapt the order to your time limitations. For example, the class may finish the Generalization Test in ten minutes. In the event that the remaining time will not permit the completion of the Discrimination of Arguments Test within the same class period, then it might be best to turn to the Interest-Values Inventory, which can be stopped in the middle if the bell rings, and continued at the next class meeting.

C. Tests A1, B1, C1, D1, and the Otis Quick-Scoring Test must be completed at one sitting. The class should not be permitted to begin any one of these tests unless there is adequate time for completing it. The approximate time required is indicated in the Manual of Directions which accompanies each test. The time allotments indicated are liberal; in most cases less time will be needed.

D. It is absolutely essential that Form 2 of the Survey of Opinions Test be administered not sooner than three days after Form 1 nor more than one week after.

E. Teachers of the experimental classes will begin teaching Lesson Unit I immediately upon completion of the testing program. The distribution of materials intended for the students in the experimental groups, such as P.E.A. test 2.5, shall be made at the discretion of each teacher, depending upon the relevance of that material to the progress of the work suggested in the lesson units.

F. The lesson units have been written for the guidance of the teachers of the experimental classes. The language used in describing the objectives is fairly precise and sometimes philosophical in nature. In the actual teaching, of course, the teacher will use simple language to convey the ideas at the students' level of comprehension. It is important to draw as much of the material as possible from the students themselves, and to avoid lecturing except where desirable in order accurately to clinch major points or principles.

G. Before taking up the work of any unit, please read carefully the material suggested under "Essential Readings." In addition to explaining the concepts involved in the units, the readings contain a wealth of illustrative material, some of which you may wish to use in class. Keep in mind the objectives of the lesson units. The procedures and the exercises and problem material furnished you are primarily illustrative and suggestive. Feel free to supplement and revise them in order to bring them into greater harmony with the interests and concerns of *your* students.

Statistics are no substitute for judgment.

—HENRY CLAY

CHAPTER IV

Presentation and Evaluation of Results

THE nature and character of the evaluation procedure to be employed in a given situation obviously depends upon the goals or objectives with respect to which achievement is to be measured. It might therefore be advisable at this point to restate briefly the objectives of this study.

It has been submitted as a fundamental assumption that one of the primary objectives of education in a democracy is to develop in young people the disposition and ability to think critically, both because it is deemed desirable for individual development as a rational and cultured human being, and because it is necessary for competent and responsible citizenship. The chief purposes of this study, stated in Chapter I, are: (1) to develop and present materials and illustrative teaching procedures which may be used effectively by the teacher of elementary,[1] secondary, and college students to stimulate growth in ability to think critically, (2) to evaluate the effectiveness of these materials and teaching procedures, and (3) to ascertain whether or not there is a relationship between ability to think critically and certain other factors, such as intelligence, test scores, age, school grades, socio-economic status, and dominant interest-values.

If the materials and illustrative teaching procedures which were developed and presented were effective in stimulating growth in ability to think critically, then certain changes which constitute evidence of the desired growth should have taken place in the boys and girls who received the special training. A first step in evaluation, then, is to define or describe the

---

[1] The present experiment was conducted at the secondary level, but modifications of the procedures have been found in practice to be effective at the upper elementary level.

behavior to be evaluated. According to the definition of critical thinking herein adopted, the objectives of the experimental teaching undertaken in this study were: (1) to cultivate in pupils an attitude of reasonableness, a disposition to consider in a thoughtful way the problems and subjects that come within the range of one's experience, (2) to help students acquire some knowledge of the methods of logical inquiry and reasoning, and (3) to help students acquire some skill in applying those methods.

A second step in evaluation is to find and describe situations in which the student will have opportunity to demonstrate his ability, and to obtain for each student a measure of initial performance. Such situations may be found in class discussion, in extracurricular activities, in relationships with other students and with teachers, in connection with written work and group activities, and in connection with the situation of responding to test items which call for knowledge of methods of logical reasoning together with some skill in applying those methods.

A third step is to get a record of what the student does when faced with situations in which he has an opportunity to demonstrate his ability. Different methods of recording are more or less suitable for appraising different kinds of behavior. Appropriate tests, interviews with pupils, teacher observation, and note-recording of pupils' classroom behavior (such as records of statements made with reference to given situations) are valuable. The making of anecdotal records, the use of various questionnaires, the study of student themes, sketches and book reviews, and the study of the student's own record of free reading also are among the useful techniques for appraising behavior.

A fourth step is the interpretation of the various measures and records in order to determine what they indicate with regard to the development, needs, attitudes, and skills of the individual student and of the class as a whole. What does the student think of his own development? What are the goals he sets for himself? What are his values? What does he think he is getting from his educational experiences, and what would he like to get?

A fifth step is to obtain final appraisals of performance which shall be approximately equivalent in form to the initial appraisals. The difference between initial and final appraisals of ability in terms of behavior is one measure of progress toward the stated objectives. It is readily conceivable, however, that some of the important effects of given educational experiences are not susceptible to appraisal, and may not be manifested in behavior until a relatively long time in the future.

A sixth step in an evaluation program might well be to ascertain what effects the educational practices employed have had upon the teacher, upon the school, and even upon the community if the students have undertaken community projects in connection with their studies. Does the teacher feel stimulated by the work? Pupils are most likely to develop the ability to think critically when the educational experience provided is stimulating for both them and the teacher.

The sources of data used for evaluation in this study are:

1. Essays from the pupils in the four experimental classes written at the end of the period of special training and testing expressing their judgment of the special training which they received.

2. Letters or papers from the teachers of the four experimental classes written six months to a year after the experiment was concluded expressing their judgment of the effectiveness of the units.

3. Expressions of opinion about the value and outcomes of the special work in critical thinking from other teachers and administrators in the schools which participated in the experiment.

4. Records of interviews and additional testing with selected pupils from the experimental group.

5. Objective records of initial and retest scores made by pupils on the Watson-Glaser Tests of Critical Thinking.

6. Objective records of retest scores on the critical thinking

tests administered six months after the conclusion of the period of special instruction.

These six methods of evaluation should furnish evidence with regard to the significant outcomes of the special training intended to help cultivate in students the disposition and ability to think critically.

EVALUATION BY TEACHERS

Teachers' Ratings

It seemed to the author reasonable to expect that after ten weeks of special work in critical thinking, the teachers of the four experimental classes ought to have well-founded impressions concerning the relative abilities manifested by their students. Consequently, a few days after the retesting had been completed, a mimeographed sheet, which is reproduced below, was sent to the teachers of the four experimental classes.

Some Kinds of Behavior Generally Associated with the Ability to Think Critically

BEHAVIOR NO 1

Does he select significant words and phrases in any statement that is important to him and ask that they be carefully defined? That is, does he show a sensitivity to vague or ambiguous words or phrases and ask just what is meant by them? For example, if someone calls another person a "radical" would he be inclined to ask what is meant by a radical—how can one tell a radical from a non-radical?

BEHAVIOR NO. 2

Does he seem to feel free to question constructively statements given by an authority, such as parents, the teacher, books, newspapers, important public figures, etc.? For example, would he be inclined to require evidence before accepting as true a statement by another student on a controversial issue to the effect that "I know this is true because my father (or teacher, or the newspaper) said so?"

BEHAVIOR NO. 3

Does he tend to require evidence in support of any conclusion he is pressed to accept? That is, will he ask for reasons or evidence when told "This is wrong," "You ought to do this," "So and so is a grafter

. . . or a communist . . . or a fascist," "Vote for me and everybody will be better off," etc.?

BEHAVIOR NO. 4

Does he try to distinguish facts from interpretation of facts? For example, suppose someone says: "According to the report of the National Resources Committee to President Roosevelt, 87% of the families in the U. S. had an income of less than $2500 during the years 1935–36. This proves that most people are too lazy or too stupid to earn more." Would the student recognize the distinction between the facts in the above statement and the interpretation which is made about the meaning of these facts? And would he be likely to recognize the implied assumption that all industrious and intelligent persons are generally able to earn more than $2500 a year?

BEHAVIOR NO. 5

Does he demonstrate the ability to see relationships between related facts and to draw warranted generalizations? For example, suppose it was a fact that a given political group was not allowed the use of a hall or auditorium in many places in a given section of the country, whereas every other political group was accorded the use of the same halls and auditoriums. Would the student be likely to make the generalization that the one group was being discriminated against in that section of the country?

BEHAVIOR NO. 6

When writing a paper, doing an assignment, or arguing for a given conclusion, does he collect and organize his facts into a coherent unit and show how his conclusion follows logically from those facts?

BEHAVIOR NO. 7

When he is organizing facts in support of an argument, point of issue, or conclusion, does he carefully take account of negative evidence in addition to the facts which support his side? Does he consider alternative possibilities in the course of arriving at a conclusion which seems soundest to him? For example, if he were trying to prove that gargling with hot water is a valuable treatment for a sore throat, would he be likely to note that some persons who do not gargle nevertheless recover?

BEHAVIOR NO. 8

Does he appear to be tolerant of new ideas and open to new evidence, even when this contradicts a belief which he holds? For example, suppose he believed that Negroes were definitely inferior to whites intellectually. His attention is then called to a well-conducted study showing that Negro children, given the same educational and environmental opportunities as white children did about as well on intelligence and school achievement tests as the white children. Would he then be inclined to change or modify his conviction that there was an innate race difference between the two groups with regard to intelligence?

The teachers were asked to list each pupil's name alphabetically in a column at the left, write across the top of the sheet numbers from one to eight corresponding to the eight kinds of behavior described, and then rate each pupil on each kind of behavior as either S (superior), A (average), P (poor), or CR (cannot rate—inadequate basis for venturing a judgment). The ratings were then transmuted into scores by assigning four points for each rating of S, two points for each rating of A, and o points for each rating of P. A rating of CR on a given kind of behavior was not counted in averaging the total number of ratings. For example:

Pupil	Class	1	2	3	4	5	6	7	8	Total Average
Adams	E1	4	CR	4	0	2	0	4	CR	2.33

For each class the teacher's ratings and total composite scores on the initial testing with the critical thinking battery were correlated. The results were as follows:

Class	r Between Teacher's Rating and Comp. Critical Thinking Score
E1	.52
E2	.48
E3	.33
E4	.40

The teacher's judgments correlated fairly well with the scores obtained by the pupils on the tests. Individual pupil differences in facility in expressing thoughts in class discussion as compared with responding to paper-and-pencil test items may, of course, have operated to color the teacher's estimates, and thereby may have tended to lower the coefficients of correlation.

*Teachers' Judgment of the Effectiveness
of the Special Training*

Some months after the conclusion of the experimental effort to train pupils to think critically, the author asked the teachers of the experimental classes to submit their own critical evaluations of the special work which they had undertaken in connection with the experiment. The teachers' evaluations are submitted as they wrote them.

Some Evaluations by Teachers of Experimental Classes

EVALUATION BY THE TEACHER OF EXPERIMENTAL CLASS EI,
AT NEWARK, NEW JERSEY

Two terms of work in the teaching of critical thinking have left me with a distinct feeling of pleasure at having taught it, and of regret at having to discontinue it. My associations with the students in the course were so much more intimate and have been so much more lasting, that, speaking only as a teacher, I feel that I received a richer reward from the course than I have from any of those in the conventional course of study. The paragraphs following may help to explain how and why.

Prior to the time that I began to read in preparation for the course, I had spent much time in the study of debating, applied logic, argumentation, and the allied arts. As a college student I had been on the debating team, and I had learned something of the methods whereby one can impale an opponent and impress a judge. I saw logic and the process of reasoning as instruments for the construction of a given case on a given side and as foils with which to parry replies.

It didn't take me long to discover that this approach was not wanted in the course outlined. The chief emphasis was to be upon the cultivation in the students of a spirit of inquiry, a spirit of regard for the weight of evidence, and a habit of open-mindedness and fairness. Questions of fact were to be decided by finding out the facts. Important subjects or questions were to be analyzed and examined critically in the light of evidence. The venturing of hypotheses and "insights" was to be encouraged, but their consequences were to be tested in practice. It was to be applied logic that operated without bias, sophistry, evasion, or ambiguity—a sober search for the vestige of truth that might be found after cautious research. My first reaction was to dismiss it all as aimless philosophizing, but my experience with the background reading and the teaching of the first unit on language convinced me of the validity of the viewpoint and of the approach I was asked to follow. And, speaking of that background reading, I found it instructive and enjoyable.

The students' first reaction to the course was one of doubtful glee. There can be no doubt that their pleasure was inspired by the novelty of taking a new type of course in which (as they were told) they were to be pioneers. The pleasure of novelty was succeeded by that of discovery, and throughout the term the opening of new fields always seemed to refresh this first delight.

Student interest, cooperation, and understanding were at a high level generally from the beginning. It was not necessary to urge the students to bring in examples; they flooded the desk with them every day. Like beginners with a microscope they wanted to examine everything and to share their findings with me and everyone else around them. They do so now, almost a year later. Even in the more formal phases of class work, they had this attitude.

In this class, the training they received was an asset. Topics were discussed and irrelevancies, *non sequiturs*, prejudices, doubtful assumptions, and unwarranted inferences were ruthlessly exposed and relegated to their proper places. The mechanics of determining probability, of sampling, of deduction, were enjoyed even in those cases where they were not fully mastered. Irrelevant points and arguments less frequently befogged the issues under discussion. Yet not all the effects of the training were desirable. Certain of the students, smaller-minded, became argumentatively arrogant; they took many subjects as natural game for logical sharpshooting. Curiously, I found more of this smart-aleck obstructionism in the brighter of my two classes.* In all fairness, though, it must be noted that such demonstrations were not well received by the rest of the class.

It did not take long for information to start trickling in from the outside which offered evidence that critical thinking was not something which students left behind in the experimental class when the bell rang. Pupils acquired an attitude of wanting evidence for assertions, together with a certain amount of analytical skill, which appeared to be general in character. Teachers began to drop remarks; they found the intrusion of the critical thinkers into their classes was a help. A teacher in the history department found that the three students in his class who were the best analysts of current events and of possible motives underlying the process of European nationalism were students who had received the special instruction in critical thinking. Two others of that department gave me vaguely complimentary reports. A member of the science department found that students who were in the experimental class in critical thinking manifested superior reasoning in the derivation of conclusions in experiments. A member of the mathematics depart-

---

* By the "brighter" class the teacher is referring to his second semester's work with a new group. Only his first class, which was "average" was included in the main experiment.

ment found that we were enriching the curriculum with our practical demonstrations on probable inferences; he said he liked the material that was being brought into his class. One result of all this was a number of applications from students who were not in the experimental class for training in critical thinking. Some of the applicants were persistent enough to ask us to provide an extra class. In addition those students in the class frequently inquired as to the chances of having a continued course; they said the training was useful in other classes.

The influence of the students' training in critical thinking extended even beyond the school. Parents were drawn into discussions and, in one case at least, enlightened. No complaints were registered. Radio material, ads, newspaper editorials, and headlines, statements of prominent citizens—all were scanned and approved or condemned, as the students felt was deserved after analysis and discussion. It was not propaganda analysis, *per se*. There was enough grist for the mill without falling back on that branch of critical thinking alone. Faulty estimates of probability, hasty generalizations, vague terminologies were watched for and detected. And I know that the students who had this training still watch for them. In my senior English classes now I have several alumni of that critical thinking group, and when discussions arise, they show the results of their training.

The course wasn't all beer and skittles; nor do I think that it was beyond improvement. Some questions and suggestions came to mind and were suggested. But the improvements themselves seemed to derive from the course's effect on me.

It seems that our students did very well in the retesting program and I don't wonder that they did. Their enthusiasm was matched by their industry. They found the work, paradoxically, difficult but pleasant. As for their teacher, he couldn't help teaching them for he was being educated himself. I look forward to the time when such a course as this will be taught not as a unit in another larger course nor as an experiment, but with the full dignity of separate class rating in the accredited curriculum, although the attitudes and skills developed should be applied and fostered in all courses and indeed in almost every area of living. A spirit of reasonableness is not something to be left behind in the classroom at three o'clock. There is no doubt, that, given a chance, such a course will accomplish its finest results; a group of inquisitive, straight thinking, fair-minded, analytical citizens-to-be.

EVALUATION BY THE TEACHER OF EXPERIMENTAL CLASS E2,
AT NEWARK, NEW JERSEY

"Critical thinking," said I, "Why I don't know how to do it, much less teach it!"

Now as I look at my experience of last year, I wonder at my temerity in approaching the work at all. In the space of three months' time, I found my attitude changed from one of indifference to one almost of affection. I had taken absolutely no previous work in the field of critical thinking. When the work was presented to me for use experimentally, I admitted to myself that I was the largest and oldest of the guinea pigs in the class.

It seems that I had always wanted the type of sharply incisive mind that I was now going to try to develop in others. I recognized its need in those situations where I sat, mouth agape, and heard or read critics, historians, economists, analysts, litterateurs, even friends, pull aside vague veils and show the way to truth in history, politics, poetry, the drama, etc. When once the veil was drawn back, I could see as they saw, that I lacked the initial perception myself. I needed the instruments of critical thinking in order to develop that degree of intellectual independence that I wanted. In a way, the course fulfilled the basic need that I had long felt.

It didn't take long to discover that my conscious need for training was matched by a greater, unconscious need in the minds of my students. They were vaguely cognizant of great minds at work, through the pages of their textbooks and their classroom experience. But they were unable to fathom what it was about men and women of history, scientists, writers, mathematicians, that permitted them to perform mental feats of analysis, deduction, induction, inference, and development far beyond the capacities of ordinary men. They didn't even realize the mental training necessary to work out a critical essay or thesis for themselves; in fact they were frequently puzzled at their inability to do so, but helpless to understand why.

The necessity for planning the units of work in the course, the varied background readings, the improvisation of problems for class use and the demand for hair-trigger responses to student questions soon provided me with a methodology in the way of approach, analysis, assortment, and exposition that often surprised me with its results. Impromptu dissections of the semantics of newspaper headlines came freely and easily as did the detection of fallacies, personal attacks, false testimonies, hasty generalizations, and stretched inferences. My own arguments were more cogently developed and more pointedly expressed than I ever hoped would be possible, not only in the "controlled monarchy" of the classroom but in the society of my friends as well.

The students' delight more than matched mine. They seemed to regard the acquisition of skills and the comprehension and application of logical principles as a sort of game. They did problems in probable inference and asked for more; they conducted a sampling census in the school lunchroom and drew numerous, varied and weird generalizations therefrom. So avidly did they scan newspapers, magazines, and books for examples of good as well as bad thinking, that I was besieged with materials, even outside of class. As one conscious epigrammatist in the class put it, "I found that not every question has two sides; it usually has five." In short, I felt that definite and specific progress had been made before my eyes in a few short weeks.

Now that a year has gone by I can gauge some advances even better. The students I had in those classes still come to me and talk about the course as if we had gone through the Argonne Forest together. One confides, "I find that critical thinking isn't too comfortable if used at home, but after all, parents are accustomed to authority." Priggish, but true. One staunch Republican told me later on that he listened to radio addresses by Democrats, however uncomfortable to him. In the lunchroom, a month ago, I overheard one of my former students pointing out very solemnly that the arguments in favor of our proposed new form of city government might easily be reduced to syllogisms. He proceeded to illustrate and then turned to me with a triumphant grin. I pointed out a fallacy in one of the syllogisms and he seemed somewhat crestfallen, for he thought he had an ironbound case. I was pleased to note that he took the corrections without resentment, an attitude I'd tried to cultivate. I could go on with incident upon incident which would show how these restless young heads dealt with hypothetical and real problems. But I think their major interest to me rests on my having experienced them and I hesitate to bore others.

I have not yet seen the full compilation of the statistical analyses of the results obtained in the experimental classes. I did examine some of the preliminary figures and some were satisfactory and some were not quite. These numbers mean little to me. They rest upon supposedly valid objective testing instruments which are said to have been reliable, but they did not measure my enjoyment in teaching the classes; they did not measure the school-wide interest in the experiment; they did not measure the innumerable extemporaneous forays into critical thinking outside of class; they did not measure the requests for admittance to another such course, if it were given; they did not measure the closeness of the associations and the degree of confidence between student and teacher that the give-and-take informality of class procedure seemed to establish. These are the gains that won't come out in graphs, and yet to me they are as important as an advance of five points in the ability to detect logical fallacies. The greatest value derived was sheer wholesome enjoyment of the study of mental processes and their application without stuffiness, without formalism, and without tears.

EVALUATION BY THE TEACHER OF EXPERIMENTAL CLASS E3,
AT NEW YORK CITY

I shall attempt here to present in retrospect only a few comments concerning my personal feelings about the experimental work in critical thinking.

1. The students enjoyed the discussion and drill material which interested them both as a good puzzle would, and as material which had current interest. They disliked the large amount of testing, which was, of course, a necessary part of the experiment.

2. There was a carry-over from the course to daily activities of the students, as far as I could judge from remarks made to me some time after the work had been completed.

3. I would have handled the material differently. The study units given to us, although interesting and valuable in detail, approximated a simplified course in logic. The approach, I felt, was too direct and too didactic. I would have preferred a course linked up even more closely with the students' lives, that would have dispensed with the syllogism and instead would have concentrated on the propaganda which is so much in evidence in our modern life. The units on prejudice and propaganda were particularly interesting because they did deal most closely with the everyday problems of the students.

EVALUATION BY THE TEACHER OF EXPERIMENTAL CLASS E4,
AT NEW YORK CITY

When I began this experiment, several qualms assailed me. I felt that the time limit for such an experiment was all too short and the material too difficult to put into teachable terms for the average high school class. I still feel that the time was entirely too short, but I am firmly convinced that this material can be taught and assimilated with undoubted value by the students.

As the work progressed, the enthusiasm of the students eased my fears and led me constantly to search for helpful devices to sustain that interest. I was pleased with their understanding of the essential nature of the work and their genuine desire to organize their thinking in a more critical fashion. It was not an unusually exuberant group, but I realized that most of the time their slowness was due to a real attempt to think through the situation which was presented to them. Too often a very active group merely hurls words and not ideas through the air.

One of the best tests of their ability was the way they handled their group discussions of their problems. One day a week was devoted to this type of discussion. As I listened in, I could very definitely observe the growth of an organized and critical approach to the subjects under discussion. The leaders exhibited marked capacity in keeping these discussions unified. Their discussions were a very practical and excellent demonstration of the results of their everyday work.

One important product of the course was the realization of the students that their lack of information continually hindered genuine critical thinking. They did a great deal more reading than classes of similar calibre.

Certainly, work of this sort should permeate the curriculum. I think this experiment points the way to a more directed and organized objective for all studies.

CLASSROOM OBSERVATION

It was noted by all the teachers of the experimental classes, as well as by the experimenter and classroom observers, that after the first few lessons on Language and Clear Thinking many students seemed to get to a stage of "confused caution" in their thinking. Having found that there was "more than appears on the surface" in the problems and class discussions during the first few lessons, they then tended to feel that there was a "catch" in almost every problem that was presented. Many of the students used indiscriminately phrases they had picked up, phrases such as "we need a definition of so-and-so," or "that's only an assumption." As the work progressed, however, and the concepts discussed became better understood, this stage of "confused caution" disappeared in most of the cases.

The work on Generalization and Probable Inference seemed to help considerably in getting over this period. This aspect of the instruction is not a necessary development so far as can be seen; probably it was a fault of the outline of the original units. In the revised units care was taken to try to obviate this difficulty; it is discussed specifically and suggestions for meeting and overcoming it are given both in the revised first unit on Language and Clear Thinking and in the last unit on Propaganda and Public Opinion. Teachers are cautioned to guard against and correct in the pupils the tendency to become skeptical or critical without being discriminating as to the content of the material.

EVALUATION BY PUPILS

At the close of the course in critical thinking the pupils in each of the participating classes were asked to write in letter or essay form a brief evaluation of the course. Each of the teachers of the experimental groups explained to the pupils that the work they had been doing during the preceding eight weeks was experimental in nature. They could contribute greatly to its improvement if they would frankly and honestly tell what they liked and what they did not like about the work, and if they could suggest any improvements. The teachers added that the students' expressions of opinions would in no way affect the grades that they would receive, and they were urged to be as critical as possible.

The classification which follows was arrived at by the author's noting down each separate idea or expression of opinion as he read the students' papers. These papers were then reread and a tally was made whenever an opinion was expressed. Both the original classification and the tally of opinion were later checked independently by two other judges, and the final classification was agreed upon in conference by the three judges (who consisted of two other persons and the author).

The opinions expressed are listed in the order of the number of times that each appeared in the students' papers. Many of the pupils may have shared several of the opinions expressed by others, even though they themselves did not state them in their own papers. The list, however, may be taken as an indication of the trend in attitude of the students toward the course.

Immediately following this list may be found samples of the students' reactions from which the classification of forty-one more or less different expressions of opinion has been compiled.

OPINIONS OR POINTS OF VIEW EXPRESSED BY STUDENTS	No. of Students Who Expressed the Given Opinion or Point of View
I liked the course very much. I found it interesting and of practical value—much better than a conventional English course.	45
I feel that this course has made me more alert to the recognition of propaganda devices frequently used in advertising, political speeches, editorials, etc., and I have learned to read editorials and listen to speeches and arguments more critically.	40
I liked the topics of prejudice and propaganda best, finding them interesting and valuable.	24
I believe our minds have been trained to think for ourselves and not to believe everything that the papers say or what we hear over the radio, or any other information until we can analyze the statements. I recognize the need for not always taking things at face value.	23
I believe that a course such as this should be both available and compulsory for all high school students.	19
I think that, in general, the course has taught us to think more clearly and more logically; I have learned to try to distinguish between fact and unsupported assertion, and have developed greater resistance to highly emotional and irrational appeals or arguments.	18
I became aware of my own prejudices (and superstitions) for the first time, and thought some funny and others crazy and unbelievable—thus becoming less prejudiced.	17
I think this study will contribute to more intelligent social living and to better citizenship. I have become more alert to problems in my environment.	17
I became aware of the need for tolerance for different and opposing points of view—to consider pros and cons of an argument or situation. I believe I became more broad-minded.	16
I liked the freedom to express opinions in class and, in general, liked the classroom discussion.	13

Opinions or Points of View Expressed by Students	No. of Students Who Expressed the Given Opinion or Point of View
I developed the habit of reflecting more before making a decision or giving an answer.	12
I recognize the importance of evidence as a rational ground for opinion or belief.	12
While I have come intellectually to appreciate my lack of basis for many personal prejudices, emotionally I still find it difficult to give them up. Prejudices which took fifteen years to build cannot be broken in three months.	11
The tests were too complicated, too long, and too boring and too many were administered at one time.	11
The course was given in too short a time; the topics were not developed thoroughly enough.	11
I liked having little homework.	10
Most of all, I enjoyed the lessons on emotionally-toned and vague words.	8
The course was too easy. It didn't give enough homework and took time from "regular" English work.	7
I learned the importance of defining abstract terms and crucial words and phrases when engaging in or listening to serious discussion.	5
Work in all my other classes has been improved.	5
The course was dull and uninteresting. It was too difficult and over our heads. I did not get much out of it.	4
I believe that the course has resulted in a marked increase in my ability to think through and handle everyday personal problems.	4
The course developed sensitivity and concern with reference to the logical soundness of what a person is saying.	4
The course was not very successful. There were a few interesting lessons . . . but for the most part it was rather silly.	3
I liked the tests. They were like doing puzzles. They involved mental gymnastics.	3

Opinions or Points of View Expressed by Students	No. of Students Who Expressed the Given Opinion or Point of View
I learned not to generalize about an entire group from the behavior of a few particular individuals in the group.	3
I came to appreciate more fully the value and importance of freedom of speech—even for those with whom we disagree.	3
I learned not to use argument against a person instead of against his argument.	3
I realized for the first time that I didn't think logically, that I made rash judgments and hasty generalizations, etc.	3
I disliked some of the questions on the Personal Data sheet and on the Opinion Test.	3
I disliked the unit involving syllogisms.	3
I am afraid of where critical thinking may lead to in terms of the undermining of long-cherished beliefs, assumptions, or values.	2
I became more critical of sources of information.	2
I learned that something which is generally true need not hold for every specific case, or need not always be true.	1
I'm not even a quarter of the way toward perfection (in critical thinking), but I'm much further along toward my goal than I was before.	1
An analysis of propaganda is largely valueless because people will get stirred up about their cherished beliefs anyway. Besides, a too critical or analytical attitude would end the enjoyment of radio programs, etc.	1
The course should have included movies, trips, etc., and more time should have been spent on newspaper work.	1
I developed the hobby of collecting advertisements.	1
The application of the questioning attitude in other classes got me into trouble.	1
I didn't understand the unit on "probability."	1
I no longer have to depend upon other people for acquiring a point of view and have therefore become much more self-assured.	1

Samples of Students' Reactions

STUDENT I

I sincerely believe the course in logic that I took this term has helped me immensely. Now I regard the things I hear and the things I read in a different light. I try to examine them logically. For instance, I try to determine whether an argument has been proven, or whether a lot of "name calling" and bad, or shall I say "deceptive," reasoning has been used, which if not examined closely seems to be perfectly valid.

One of the most common of the illogical practices—prejudices—was discussed and analyzed. Although my teacher had a hard time convincing me how unfounded my prejudices were, she can be assured that she has succeeded in most every case.

I believe in practical education. The study of logic, in my mind, is very practical; I therefore would suggest that it be taught on a much larger scale in the school system—not as an experiment but as a regular course.

STUDENT 2

Critical thinking has helped me examine advertisements, newspaper articles, and editorials, and not to believe everything I read or hear. In finding the assumptions in various advertisements, it has helped me to understand how a thing can be implied and how it can lead me to believe something that really is false. I also know now the value of definitions, not merely "glittering generalities. . . ." I have discovered my prejudices and have tried to overcome them, although I have not been successful in many cases. Propaganda cannot sway my opinion as rapidly as it may have done before. . . . Both sides of the question must be considered before I form my opinions.

STUDENT 3

This term, instead of taking regular English, I became, together with forty-seven others, a human guinea pig. . . .

I think I have learned not to take things at their face value and not to be taken in by propaganda. However, I think sometimes I dig too deep and get myself into an awful lot of trouble.

And, of course, very often I begin to ask the whys and wherefores of things at the wrong time and place.

This scientific method we learn about seems so right and so much better than any other kind of reasoning that I am inclined to try to find faults with it. Everytime I think I have proved something is wrong with it, I find that I have made an error in reasoning or else I find that I have "insufficient data." Of course, the merits of a scientific method become more and more plain to me everytime I do this, but it does "get my goat," as the saying goes.

Then, too, a scientific method has destroyed so many of my pet beliefs that I can't help disliking it slightly even though I fully realize all of its good points.

Naturally once in a while (like everything else) this course becomes boring and there are times when I don't fully understand just what is meant (except that it has to do with clear thinking). . . . In spite of these faults I believe that every student should take this course because he will get something out of it. And I think this course is preferable to almost all other English courses, because it really concerns us, and it is nearer to our everyday lives than any other subject.

STUDENT 4

When I grow up, I'll be able to vote more intelligently, not just pick out a candidate who resorts to calling his opponents names or some candidate who makes a simply lovely speech and the audience doesn't know what he is talking about.

We were taught to think straight, to use logic in our reasoning. When arguing we should always consider our opponent's point of view and, if he is right, be ready to change our opinion. Not to go in for hasty generalization, assuming that if one person of a certain race does something bad the whole race is dangerous. Not to suppose if anything is generally true it has to be true in every single case. . . . Not to believe a statement true unless we have sufficient evidence to prove the truth of the statement. Not to criticize the man we argue with, but to criticize his arguments.

. . . It is good to cultivate the habit of suspended judgment and consideration of alternative possibilities. . . .

STUDENT 5

I am still prejudiced. These prejudices I have were built in many years, and they cannot be shaken easily. I am trying, however, to overcome them.

STUDENT 6

The discussion on logic, prejudice, and propaganda has left a distinct impression in my mind. It has opened an entirely new line of understanding and has aided me in making many decisions. . . .

STUDENT 7

This course has helped me to recognize my many prejudices and their causes, chiefly my home life. Since there is very little I can do about my home life, the only way I can overcome the prejudices is by being more open-minded in the future and looking at the question from both sides. . . .

STUDENT 8

I think that the course should have been twice as long as it was in order to make us understand its principles to a much greater extent. . . .

STUDENT 9

I don't believe this course will have any lasting effects on the students since there was not sufficient time to cover each topic thoroughly. The tests should not have been given one right after the other. . . .

STUDENT 10

The series of tests became meaningless and monotonous after a time. They become just like ordinary tests, instead of thoughtful, logical questions to be done in full earnestness. . . .

STUDENT 11

I think the experiments should have been tried on college students instead of on high school students. . . .

STUDENT 12

It has made me more self-assured, because it has made me realize that I cannot be bullied into accepting anybody's opinion, by means of harsh words or loud tones. I realize now that it is the argument and the facts or assumptions on which it is based that really count. I no longer accept an argument at face value. I think too, that I have acquired a much broader conception of world affairs by recognizing and evaluating propaganda to a much higher degree than I did before.

STUDENT 13

Clear thinking has also helped me in many of my subjects in school, especially algebra which requires a great deal of logical thinking. Through careful reasoning in many problems, it has been easier for me this year than last. I think some of this is due to my course in logical thinking. Open-mindedness, as I said before, has also helped to give me a clearer understanding of history, which had previously been hampered by social and religious prejudices.

EVALUATION BY INTERVIEWS

About six weeks after the pupil participation in the experiment was finished and the test papers had been scored and differences between initial and final testings calculated and tabulated, interviews were arranged with twenty-four of the pupils who were chosen for interview because of one of the following reasons: (1) The student was one of those whose score gain between the two tests was highest; (2) the student was one of those whose score gain was lowest; (3) the student made an approximately average gain; (4) the student had a relatively low I. Q. but gained very much more than the mean number of points; (5) the student had a relatively high I. Q. but gained less than the mean number of points; (6) the student was in the control group but nevertheless gained more than the mean number of points gained by those in the experimental group.[2]

The interviews were initiated by general discussion of the experiment. The interviewer then went over with the student some of his answers to items on the critical thinking tests, inquiring *why* he answered as he did in each instance—initial and retest. The interviewer inquired about those items which had been answered correctly as well as those items which had been answered incorrectly, but he touched especially on items which had been answered differently on the initial and on the final test.

Following are excerpts from some of the interview records and a summary of the main trends which these records reveal. For purposes of subsequent reference it might be noted here that the initial mean composite total score for the experimental group on the battery of critical thinking tests was 350.39 and the retest score after instruction was 428.15. The initial mean I. Q. for the experimental group was 106.60 and the retest mean I. Q. 109.66.

[2] The interviews were conducted by the author and by an assistant who had her master's degree in psychology and who had had six months of clinical training under supervision at an educational clinic connected with a school of education at the college she attended.

Excerpts from Interview Records

BOY. Class: E1. Initial I.Q.: 107. Initial composite: 303. Retest composite: 332. Gain: 29 points.

In response to the examiner's first question concerning his opinion of the course, Edwin said: "Well, I didn't think so carefully the first time I took the tests as the second time. The course taught me to think more carefully before coming to a conclusion. The first time I took this test I put down whatever came into my head at first thought, but the second time I thought the problem over. I think, though, that I have forgotten a lot of the things I learned in the course."

Edwin was asked to explain his reasoning on several items in Test B–AR which he answered differently on the test and retest. It appeared that one of his chief difficulties both on this and on the Discrimination of Arguments Test was to keep in mind that the premises (in test B–AR), and the arguments (in Test E) were to be accepted as true. Once he realized that he was to accept the premises or arguments as true, his reasoning was much more accurate. In general, Edwin seemed to have grasped some of the specific emphases of the training, but he did not manifest a clear understanding of the general principles involved in logical thinking.

BOY. Class: E4. Initial I.Q.: 104. Initial composite: 372. Retest composite: 355. Loss: 17 points.

Albert said he felt that the course had changed his general attitude and made him more tolerant and open-minded. In several instances in which Albert had answered an item differently on the two administrations of the test, he appeared to have no tenable basis for either answer, and in general exhibited little understanding of the processes of logical reasoning. Albert appeared to have developed a disposition to ask for evidence for assertions, but little competence to distinguish between relevant and irrelevant reasons in support of a given point of view.

BOY. Class: E3. Initial I.Q.: 100. Initial composite: 433. Retest composite: 499. Gain: 66 points.

In response to the interviewer's question, Victor said: "I'm not saying this just because I think you want to hear it. I really think the course is swell. After I took the tests I discussed them with my family. I never was interested in the regular English course that we had every term and I thought that the course was a good change. We studied very interesting material, and I use everything I learned now, too. The course also helped me outside of school. I developed a skepticism, and I don't believe everything I read now just because it is something in print; I want to know on what grounds the authority for the article or statement is said to be true."

Among the questions which the interviewer asked pertaining to the tests was the following:

Q.: On one of the tests you said that most gamblers are superstitious, and on the other you said you don't know how many gamblers are superstitious. Which of these answers do you agree with now, and why?

A.: I said most on the first test because I thought of a few people I knew personally, but after I took the course I realized that I didn't knew enough gamblers to make a statement as to how many were or were not superstitious.

The following dialogue appears on the interview record:

Q.: In support of the argument (from the Discrimination of Arguments Test) that "Communists should be barred from public office," you said the following argument was *weak,* and at another time you said it was *strong.* "If we allowed Communists to hold public office, it would be the same as allowing Russia a voice in our government, since the Communists take their orders from Russia." What do you think now, and why?

A.: Well, I don't know enough about the Communists in order to say whether that statement is true or not, but if I accept it as true, then I think it is a strong argument because that certainly is a good reason for keeping Communists out of office.

On every one of the tests Victor revealed good reasoning, open-mindedness, and a tolerant attitude. At the end of the interview he stated: "Now that I have taken the course I have learned how to state the reasons for my beliefs much more clearly."

GIRL. Class: E2. Initial I.Q.: 93. Initial composite: 346. Retest composite: 505. Gain: 159 points.

In response to the first question Ruth said: "I honestly think that the course helped me a great deal. I liked it a lot and wish I could take it again."

The interviewer asked Ruth for her reasoning with reference to eighteen of the test items, three from each test. In every instance the reason which she gave for her answer was logically correct. For example:

Q.: Accept as true the following statement. "After I took two bottles of Flubdub I felt better than I had for years. There is no doubt that Flubdub has done wonders for me." Does the conclusion given necessarily follow the statement? Or doesn't it? And in either case, why?

A.: The answer is no. The Flubdub may have helped him but it could have been exercising or fresh air or any number of other things. The inference does not necessarily follow.

BOY. Class E4. Initial I. Q.: 119. Initial composite: 336. Retest composite: 492. Gain: 156 points.

In response to the first question Abe said: "Well, first I think that the students should not have been told that the course was an experiment because they thought of it as a snap course, and therefore didn't do as much work as they might have done otherwise. I also think that the course was not given over a long enough period of time. We should have had much more time of actual work than to have wasted so much time taking the tests. We also got very tired of taking so many tests. But anyhow I think this course has helped me a great deal personally. I found that I could apply many of the things I learned to my history and economics classes. I sometimes interrupt the lessons now to ask the teacher for his reasons in support of some of the things he asserts. I really feel much smarter since taking the course."

When Abe was shown some of the items he answered differently on the initial test and the retest, he was able to explain the correct reasons satisfactorily in almost every case. When the interviewer asked him why he answered as he did the first time, his most frequent response was: "I can't see how I could have answered that way the first time. My thinking is so set along logical lines now that I can't remember how I thought before."

In summary, the interviews revealed a close correspondence between ability in critical thinking as manifested by the student's retest score and ability to explain coherently during the interview the reasons for his answers to the test items. Desirable outcomes, such as the development of attitudes of open-mindedness, tolerance, and regard for evidence were revealed.

The chief sources of errors in reasoning as revealed by the students' explanation of why they answered as they did are:

1. Failure or inability to understand the general guiding principles underlying the correct solution of the problem.

2. Failure or inability to comprehend the meaning of what they read (in the test item).

3. Failure to discriminate between more and less pertinent considerations in a complex situation.

4. Unique interpretations of the meaning of a question or an argument. The source of error noted here appears to be similar to that noted by Duncker [90], Devnich [80], and Chant [52], who believe that previously conceived relation-

ships to given material (or a given situation) will persist and prevent the viewing of the material in terms of new relationships, thus keeping the subject from gaining the solution to the problem. This is similar to the explanation of errors in terms of the inflexibility of the reasoner's set. Sometimes the "error" involved in this connection may not really be an error at all, but rather a case of difficulty which may arise in communication between persons who do not have similar connotations for certain words, phrases, or statements.

5. Inability to keep in mind the direction: "For purposes of this test regard each argument as true," or, "Although the premises as stated may or may not be true, for the purpose of this test you are to *assume* they are true, and to judge whether the conclusions drawn from the premises are sound or unsound."

6. Inability to keep wishes from influencing interpretation of data or evaluation of arguments.

7. A tendency to make unwarranted sweeping generalizations on the basis of limited personal experience.

8. Failure or inability to pay attention or to make a serious effort to obtain a correct solution.

9. Emotional factors such as over-anxiety, nervousness.

The technique of asking the individual pupil to explain how he arrived at his answers to given problems with which he has been presented affords a simple and useful means for gaining insight into his reasoning processes. Educational attempts to develop ability to think critically might well be more fruitful if a diagnosis is first made of the methods of reasoning habitually employed by each pupil in problem-solving.

EVALUATION BY STATISTICAL TREATMENT OF RESULTS OF THE TESTING PHASE OF THE EXPERIMENT

Comparison of Mean Gains of Experimental and Control Groups on Critical Thinking Tests

Table 3 shows the initial and retest scores on the Watson-Glaser Tests of Critical Thinking of each of the experimental

TABLE 3

MEAN GAINS OF EXPERIMENTAL AND CONTROL CLASSES ON THE WATSON-GLASER TESTS (TOTAL COMPOSITE Z SCORE)

Group N		City	INITIAL TEST			FINAL TEST			Change
			Range	Mean	S. D.	Range	Mean	S. D.	
E1	25	Newark	171–354	267.44	65.79	257–439	345.16	55.23	70.72
E2	29	Newark	228–425	305.41	42.31	278–456	374.00	40.64	68.49
E3	32	N. Y.	197–444	309.91	47.77	300–502	385.44	44.91	75.53
E4	41	N. Y.	205–403	307.07	41.15	272–489	370.73	50.12	63.66
Compos. E127			171–444	299.61	51.85	257–502	370.15	49.82	71.08
C1	30	Newark	213–402	294.87	52.06	187–460	331.47	68.70	36.60
C2	30	Newark	171–374	295.67	51.07	228–428	347.60	58.24	50.93
C3	37	N. Y.	217–419	318.68	49.67	213–476	356.22	51.92	37.54
C4	35	N. Y.	201–395	281.94	37.16	248–427	321.54	39.76	39.62
Compos. C132			171–419	298.52	48.94	187–476	339.44	56.68	40.90
Diff. E-C	30.16								
Diff./σ_d	6.09								

and control classes. The table also shows the composite scores of the four experimental classes considered as one experimental group, as compared with the four control classes considered as one control group. Each student's total critical thinking score was calculated by converting the score obtained on each of the six tests in the Watson-Glaser series into the Hull modification of Z-scale units, and then obtaining the sum. The procedure for transmuting raw scores into Hull Z-scores is indicated below.

M = the mean of the distribution of scores on the given test
σ = the standard deviation of the distribution of scores on given test
X_1 = the individual's score on the given test
50 = the mean of the converted series
14 = the standard deviation of the converted series
X = the individual's score in the converted series
$S = \dfrac{14}{\sigma}$, and $K = 50 - MS$; Then $X = K + SX_1$

The mean gain of the experimental group over the control group is statistically significant. The smallest gain among the experimental classes, 63.66 points, is greater than the largest gain among the control classes, which is 50.93 points. It will be noted, however, that control class C2 gained 11.33 points more than did class C4, which showed the next largest gain among the controls. The teacher of class C2 had made a special effort to develop in the students what he termed "the habit of reflective reading." He devoted one day a week to outlining, analyzing, and summarizing with his students selected articles from the *Reader's Digest*. This work also involved study of concepts in language comprehension similar to those discussed in Lesson Unit 1, Language and Clear Thinking, developed in connection with this experiment.

The statistical technique used in this study to ascertain the significance of differences between mean gains is indicated in the illustration below for Test D, Generalization (Table 9).

Group	N	Mean Gain between Test-Retest	$N\sigma^2$ Gains*
E1	25	12.96	3100.96
E2	29	11.40	1970.69
E3	32	15.35	8613.22
E4	41	11.03	5256.98
	127	Compos. M = 12.59	Q = 18941.85
C1	30	7.65	3089.97
C2	30	10.07	3441.37
C3	37	2.86	3515.82
C4	35	5.11	7183.04
	132	Compos. M = 6.19	R = 17230.20

$$\frac{Q + R}{251} = \frac{36172.05}{251} = \sigma_T^2 = 144.11$$

$$\sigma_{M_E}^2 = \frac{\sigma_T^2}{127} = \frac{144.11}{127} = 1.13 \quad \text{and} \quad \sigma_{M_C}^2 = \frac{\sigma_T^2}{132} = \frac{144.11}{132} = 1.09$$

$$\sigma_{M_E - M_C} = \frac{Q + R}{251} \times \sqrt{\frac{1}{127} + \frac{1}{132}} = 1.49$$

$$\frac{d}{d} = \frac{d}{\sigma_{M_E - M_C}} = \frac{12.59 - 6.19}{1.49} = 4.30$$

* The $N\sigma^2$ gains are obtained by finding σ^2 and multiplying by N. Thus $\sigma^2 = \frac{\Sigma x^2}{N} - M^2_x$, where x^2 is the square of the gains (or losses) in score between test and retest of each member of the group.

Table 4 shows the distribution of gains (and losses) in total composite score for both the experimental and control groups on the tests of critical thinking.

TABLE 4

DISTRIBUTION OF GAINS IN TOTAL COMPOSITE CRITICAL
THINKING SCORE FOR THE EXPERIMENTAL
AND CONTROL GROUPS

Gain (in score points)	Midpoint	(Exper. Group) Frequency N = 127	(Control Group) Frequency N = 132
170– 179.9	175	0	1
160– 169.9	165	2	0
150– 159.9	155	2	0
140– 149.9	145	1	1
130– 139.9	135	4	0
120– 129.9	125	5	0
110– 119.9	115	7	1
100– 109.9	105	10	1
90– 99.9	95	9	7
80– 89.9	85	12	7
70– 79.9	75	9	6
60– 69.9	65	9	15
50– 59.9	55	15	10
40– 49.9	45	13	17
30– 39.9	35	11	20
20– 29.9	25	5	12
10– 19.9	15	8	9
0– 9.9	5	3	12
0– – 9.9	– 5	0	7
– 10– – 19.9	– 15	1	2
– 20– – 29.9	– 25	0	1
– 30– – 39.9	– 35	1	1
– 40– – 49.9	– 45	0	1
– 50– – 59.9	– 55	0	1

Mean	70.54	40.92	
90th percentile	122.60	86.86	
73rd percentile	96.34	62.24	
27th percentile	44.07	21.36	
10th percentile	19.90	.17	

Tables 5 to 11 show the initial and retest raw scores of the experimental and control classes on each of the Watson-Glaser tests.[3]

[3] The possible range of scores on each of these tests of critical thinking is from 0–100 except in the case of Test F (Evaluation of Arguments), upon which the maximum score is 96 and a minus-sign score is possible.

TABLE 5

MEAN GAINS OF EXPERIMENTAL AND CONTROL CLASSES ON ATTITUDE
SCORE*—TEST A (A SURVEY OF OPINIONS)

Group	N	INITIAL TEST			FINAL TEST			Change
		Range	Mean	S. D.	Range	Mean	S. D.	
E_1	25	39–95	64.12	11.44	44–95	69.52	12.25	5.40
E_2	29	48–74	62.59	6.12	54–90	71.55	8.08	8.96
E_3	32	54–85	70.28	9.25	54–97	73.84	10.38	3.56
E_4	41	45–91	69.85	9.25	47–97	72.12	10.36	2.27
Compos. E	127	39–95	67.18	9.74	44–97	71.91	10.41	4.74
C_1	30	48–93	67.27	10.49	44–96	69.40	10.90	2.13
C_2	30	44–87	65.70	9.20	38–91	65.20	12.31	− .50
C_3	37	54–98	73.49	10.55	42–95	73.89	11.39	.40
C_4	35	52–81	64.00	7.45	55–91	68.63	8.43	4.63
Compos. C	132	44–98	67.79	10.33	38–96	69.50	11.81	1.71

Diff. E-C   3.03
Diff. $/\sigma_d$ 3.44

* The attitude score on Test A is not a measure of critical thinking; only the consistency score from this test is counted in obtaining the total composite critical thinking score.

TABLE 6

MEAN GAINS OF EXPERIMENTAL AND CONTROL CLASSES ON CONSISTENCY
SCORE—TEST A (A SURVEY OF OPINIONS)

Group	N	INITIAL TEST			FINAL TEST			Change
		Range	Mean	S. D.	Range	Mean	S. D.	
E_1	25	52–95	81.16	10.68	60–100	84.16	9.57	3.00
E_2	29	67–97	85.00	5.93	64–100	88.00	7.35	3.00
E_3	32	70–97	87.41	6.11	76–100	90.38	7.34	2.97
E_4	41	74–99	87.34	6.19	68–100	88.30	8.48	.96
Compos. E	127	52–99	85.61	7.63	60–100	87.94	8.53	2.33
C_1	30	62–99	83.27	8.18	48–100	78.60	12.67	− 4.67
C_2	30	52–97	82.00	9.24	64–100	84.14	9.20	2.14
C_3	37	74–100	88.68	7.46	76–100	90.38	5.82	1.70
C_4	35	67–97	84.46	8.01	68–100	85.72	7.83	1.26
Compos. C	132	52–100	84.81	8.59	48–100	85.05	9.96	.24

Diff. E-C   2.09
Diff. $/\sigma_d$ 1.94

TABLE 7

MEAN GAINS OF EXPERIMENTAL AND CONTROL CLASSES
ON TEST B–AR (LOGICAL REASONING)

Group	N	INITIAL TEST			FINAL TEST			Change
		Range	Mean	S. D.	Range	Mean	S. D.	
E1	25	36–76	56.68	11.79	52–100	76.80	11.92	20.12
E2	29	44–96	64.52	11.49	60–96	81.38	10.78	16.86
E3	32	28–96	52.63	14.25	36–100	73.75	12.49	21.12
E4	41	32–84	52.32	13.85	52–100	70.73	11.89	18.41
Compos. E	127	28–96	57.05	13.81	36–100	75.12	12.48	18.07
C1	30	36–96	58.13	15.69	32–96	64.33	16.08	6.20
C2	30	40–84	63.20	13.40	44–96	68.33	16.28	5.13
C3	37	40–80	57.62	11.66	52–92	69.30	10.56	11.68
C4	35	36–96	55.83	13.54	32–100	63.09	12.69	7.26
Compos. C	132	36–96	58.53	13.81	32–100	66.30	14.14	7.77

Diff. E–C 11.19
Diff./σ_d 7.01

TABLE 8

MEAN GAINS OF EXPERIMENTAL AND CONTROL CLASSES
ON TEST C (INFERENCE)

Group	N	INITIAL TEST			FINAL TEST			Change
		Range	Mean	S. D.	Range	Mean	S. D.	
E1	25	24–70	55.12	9.77	32–76	62.64	8.67	7.52
E2	29	38–84	58.48	9.52	44–86	67.10	9.52	8.62
E3	32	44–82	62.25	8.54	52–84	68.63	6.13	6.38
E4	41	36–74	58.00	9.72	42–88	63.56	8.70	5.56
Compos. E	127	24–84	58.61	9.71	32–88	65.46	8.68	6.85
C1	30	26–78	57.40	12.40	42–80	65.93	10.43	8.53
C2	30	34–74	54.60	11.43	34–76	62.50	11.16	7.90
C3	37	26–78	55.30	11.44	32–84	61.98	11.34	6.68
C4	35	26–62	50.52	9.89	30–74	57.49	9.93	6.97
Compos. C	132	26–78	54.35	11.56	30–84	61.81	11.14	7.46

Diff. E–C   .61
Diff./σ_d *

* Not significant.

TABLE 9

MEAN GAINS OF EXPERIMENTAL AND CONTROL CLASSES
ON TEST D (GENERALIZATION)

Group	N	INITIAL TEST			FINAL TEST			Change
		Range	Mean	S. D.	Range	Mean	S. D.	
E1	25	27–69	49.32	10.74	50–80	62.28	8.23	12.96
E2	29	39–69	57.31	8.09	55–90	68.71	8.21	11.40
E3	32	42–96	56.59	12.66	45–95	71.94	12.34	15.35
E4	41	32–84	62.17	9.83	42.5–100	73.20	10.62	11.03
Compos. E	127	27–96	57.12	11.38	42.5–100	69.71	10.94	12.59
C1	30	36–72	56.90	9.91	46–82.5	64.55	10.15	7.65
C2	30	36–75	58.60	9.32	55–87.5	68.67	7.65	10.07
C3	37	42–84	65.52	9.92	50–87	68.38	8.36	2.86
C4	35	39–75	57.17	9.32	42.5–87.5	62.28	11.62	5.11
Compos. C	132	36–84	59.77	9.64	42.5–87.5	65.96	9.97	6.19

Diff. E–C 6.40
Diff./σ_d 4.30

TABLE 10

MEAN GAINS OF EXPERIMENTAL AND CONTROL CLASSES
ON TEST E (DISCRIMINATION OF ARGUMENTS)

Group	N	INITIAL TEST			FINAL TEST			Change
		Range	Mean	S. D.	Range	Mean	S. D.	
E1	25	42.5–77.5	62.20	9.06	47.5–95	67.56	11.01	5.36
E2	29	42.5–87.5	63.62	10.70	47.5–95	68.97	10.88	5.35
E3	32	40–87.5	66.86	9.92	50–92.5	71.50	9.95	4.64
E4	41	47.5–85	63.11	8.29	55–90	70.37	8.84	7.26
Compos. E	127	40–87.5	63.99	9.61	47.5–95	69.78	10.15	5.79
C1	30	45–80	62.42	9.16	50–85	68.42	10.45	6.00
C2	30	42.5–82.5	63.88	10.53	47.5–90	69.65	11.23	5.77
C3	37	45–82.5	65.34	9.55	42.5–100	69.04	11.54	3.70
C4	35	45–77.5	63.34	8.01	50–90	69.57	8.73	6.23
Compos. C	132	42.5–82.5	63.81	9.52	42.5–100	69.18	10.55	5.37

Diff. E–C .42
Diff./σ_d *

* Not significant.

TABLE 11

MEAN GAINS OF EXPERIMENTAL AND CONTROL CLASSES
ON TEST F (EVALUATION OF ARGUMENTS)

Group	N	INITIAL TEST			FINAL TEST			Change
		Range	Mean	S. D.	Range	Mean	S. D.	
E1	25	−7–66	26.72	17.95	3–84	45.72	22.53	19.00
E2	29	4–76	31.28	19.54	3–90	47.38	21.05	16.10
E3	32	0–63	35.91	16.73	12–75	53.25	15.03	17.34
E4	41	4–87	36.98	17.37	6–96	52.66	18.82	15.68
Compos. E	127	−7–87	33.39	18.28	3–96	50.24	19.56	16.85
C1	30	3–71	34.60	18.41	3–84	45.93	23.44	11.33
C2	30	6–75	31.63	15.94	3–84	44.77	23.12	13.14
C3	37	8–100	36.87	24.80	3–72	43.87	20.05	7.00
C4	35	0–69	27.71	16.42	3–75	32.74	18.91	5.03
Compos. C	132	0–100	33.02	19.71	3–84	41.59	21.97	8.57

Diff. E–C 7.99
Diff./σ_d 3.44

The gain of the experimental over the control group was found to be statistically significant on the battery of critical thinking tests (Table 3) and on Tests B–AR, D, and F. On Test A (consistency score) the difference divided by the standard deviation of the difference was found to be 1.94, which means that there are 97 chances in 100 that the true significance is greater than zero. The diff/σ_d for Tests A (attitude), B–AR, D, and F was in each case more than 3.00, which implies almost with certainty that the true difference is greater than zero. While the attitude score on Test A is not considered a measure of critical thinking, it is interesting to note that a statistically significant gain (Table 5) in the direction of "progressive" as opposed to "reactionary" views on certain controversial public issues occurred among the students in the experimental group.

The gain of the experimental group over the control group on Test E was .42. This gain is not statistically significant. On Test C, the control group gained 7.46 points on the retest, while the experimental group gained only 6.85 points. Apparently the special instruction given the experimental group was not successful in developing ability to distinguish properly between the five categories of inference as measured by Test C, or between strong and weak arguments as measured by Test E. Jewett [147], in his study, reports that the class he taught did make statistically significant gains on Test C, but he too found that his experimental group did not improve significantly over the control group on Test E.

After the retesting had been completed, the author went over with some of the students their responses to the items on the tests, and asked their reasons for answering as they did. In several instances students indicated difficulty in keeping in mind the directions for Test E, which requested that for purposes of the test, the subject was to regard each argument as true and then decide whether he would call it strong or weak. Jewett reports the same difficulty and believes that this probably is the chief cause of the insignificant gain on Test E after instruction in critical thinking. In the 1940 edition of the tests an effort was made to reduce this difficulty by repeating the directions at the bottom of each page of the test booklet.

The evidence from previous research (Fawcett's study [99], for instance) indicates that abilities of the kind measured by Tests C and E can be improved by instruction if those abilities are taught for consciously and specifically, and if appropriate practice problems and exercises are provided and explained to the pupils. There was no material in the original lesson units devoted specifically to explaining the logical processes involved or providing practice in distinguishing strong from weak arguments, as required in Test E. Nor was there any material devoted specifically to training pupils to discriminate between the five categories of inference found in Test C. Other factors which may be related to the lack of significant improvement on Tests C and E will be considered when the intercorrelations among the tests are presented and discussed.

The fact that there was not more marked improvement in consistency score (Test A), which is a measure of freedom from the tendency to support mutually exclusive views on given questions, may be accounted for in part by the fact that consistency scores on this test were relatively high on the initial test. The initial mean consistency score among the experimental students was 85.61 out of a possible maximum of 100. There was not as much "room for improvement" on this test as there was on each of the other tests in the battery.

The fact that the gain of the experimental group on some of the tests was statistically significant while on other tests it was not significant may be an indication that in addition to the possible contributory factors discussed above, the abilities measured by the different tests tend to develop at varying rates and are different in their susceptibility to improvement after a short period of instruction. Such a hypothesis is supported by Downing's study [86], reported in Chapter II. Further support of this interpretation is offered by the teachers of the experimental classes who report that it was relatively easy, for instance, to get students to see the possibilities of errors involved in hasty generalizations and sweeping conclusions on the basis of too limited experience, but relatively difficult to make clear the concept of probable inference based on evidence of varying adequacy, taken up in Unit 2, Generalization and Probable Inference. Table 13 (page 143) shows that the Inference Test (C) is more closely correlated with intelligence than any of the other tests, which further accounts for the lack of significant gain on this test after ten weeks' instruction.

Comparison of Mean Gains of Experimental and Control Groups on Otis Quick-Scoring Mental Ability Test

Were the abilities measured by the Otis Quick-Scoring Mental Ability Test improved by the special instruction given to the pupils in the experimental classes? Did the pupils in the experimental classes gain more than the pupils in the control classes in whatever is measured by a "general intelligence" test like the Otis? Table 12 presents the initial and retest intelligence test scores of the four experimental and four control classes.

TABLE 12

MEAN GAINS OF EXPERIMENTAL AND CONTROL CLASSES ON THE OTIS
QUICK-SCORING TEST OF MENTAL ABILITY†

Group	N	INITIAL TEST			FINAL TEST			Change
		Range	Mean	S. D.	Range	Mean	S. D.	
E1	25	23–54	41.88	8.33	29–66	48.08	9.15	6.20
E2	29	30–60	43.31	8.07	28–55	44.48	9.55	1.17
E3	32	34–74	48.00	8.64	35–79	52.31	9.02	4.31
E4	41	25–67	43.59	9.04	31–70	49.12	9.36	5.53
Compos. E	127	23–74	44.30	8.83	28–79	48.66	9.67	4.36
C1	30	22–58	41.70	9.81	26–68	44.63	10.35	2.93
C2	30	27–68	46.13	10.63	27–74	50.83	10.48	4.70
C3	37	22–66	47.95	11.46	31–71	51.70	9.73	3.75
C4	35	28–61	42.60	8.47	25–63	45.69	7.87	3.09
Compos. C	132	22–68	44.70	10.49	25–74	48.30	10.09	3.60

Diff. E–C   .76
Diff./σ_d *

† The scores reported in this table are in raw score points.
* Not significant.

The gain of the experimental group on the Otis test of .76
of a raw score point more than the gain of the control group is
negligible and not statistically significant. The units of work
in critical thinking, then, did not result in any appreciable improvement in ability to get higher scores on the Otis Intelligence test. There is evidence, however, presented under the
headings "Evaluation by Teachers" and "Evaluations by
Pupils," that the units of work in critical thinking did help to
develop in a considerable number of students what might be
called "gains in the manifestation of intelligent behavior."

Incidentally, it is not difficult to train pupils to gain in
retest scores on a given intelligence test if it is desired to coach
them for that purpose. Research on the effects of coaching
pupils with items similar to those in a given intelligence test
reveals that it is easy to raise retest scores on that given test
by such coaching, although the gains tend to be temporary
[Chen, 54]. While the subjects so coached gain in skill to

respond properly to the relationships or problems presented in the given test, there is no evidence of appreciable growth in general ability to behave intelligently, or even in ability to make higher scores on other intelligence tests composed of problems of a different type from those studied. If such growth did result from coaching with material similar to the material contained in given intelligence tests, then a most valuable kind of educational material would be available. The gains from the work in critical thinking are more significant and more subtle than just temporary pencil-and-paper test gains. The relationship and differences between the abilities measured by the Otis test and by the critical thinking tests will be discussed in a later section of this chapter.

Intercorrelations among Test Scores

Table 13 shows the intercorrelations among the critical thinking tests for both the initial and the final testing, and the correlation between the critical thinking tests and other measures, such as average school grades and reading test scores. Table 14 shows the correlations between initial and retest scores on tests which were administered twice to the experimental group.

On the whole, the intercorrelations obtained from the retest scores were fairly similar to those obtained from the initial scores. It is interesting to note that in every instance the retest correlation was higher than the corresponding initial correlation with the component critical thinking score (see Table 13, Column 11). This suggests that the aspects of critical thinking measured by the tests tend to fuse after training into a more highly integrated and organized pattern so that the individual is better able to bring to bear upon a problem the methods and processes of logical inquiry and critical thinking. The evidence for this hypothesis, however, is not adequate to warrant its acceptance. Low correlations remained low and relatively high correlations remained high, except in the case of Test F, which correlated .28 with the initial composite scores and .49 with the retest composite.

TABLE 13

CORRELATION TABLE (EXPERIMENTAL GROUP: N = 127)

	1 School Marks*	2 N.D. Total	3 Otis I / Otis II	4 A Att.I / A Att.II	5 A Cons.I / A Cons.II	6 B-AR I / B-AR II	7 C I / C II	8 D I / D II	9 E I / E II	10 F I / F II	11 Comp.I / Comp.II
School Marks	—	.47	.35 / .31	.57 / .57	.22 / .35	.21 / .10	.13 / .16	.02 / .06	.24 / .26	.52 / .51	.06 / .12
N.D. Reading	.47	—	.69 / .71	.47 / .28	.17 / .22	.14 / .32	.55 / .47	-.06 / -.15	.28 / .43	.50 / .42	.32 / .36
Otis I	.35	.69	—	.44	.27	.34	.52	.03	.14	.41	.46
Otis II	.31	.71	—	.19	.19	.37	.51	.19	.30	.43	.48
A Att. I	.37	.47	.44	—	.37	.14	.35	.03	.23	.36	.36
A Att. II	.57	.28	.19	—	.52	.21	.21	.07	.22	.45	.41
A Cons. I	.22	.17	.27	.37	—	.13	.17	.25	.16	.09	.30
A Cons. II	.35	.22	.19	.52	—	.13	.28	.27	.08	.24	.31
B-AR I	.21	.14	.34	.14	.13	—	.21	.01	.18	.19	.21
B-AR II	.10	.32	.37	.21	.13	—	.35	.12	.35	.31	.30
C I	.13	.55	.52	.35	.17	.21	—	.09	.21	.42	.45
C II	.16	.47	.51	.21	.28	.35	—	.08	.38	.47	.51
D I	.02	-.06	.03	.03	.25	.01	.09	—	.12	.01	.20
D II	.06	-.15	.19	.07	.27	.12	.08	—	.11	.20	.24
E I	.24	.28	.14	.23	.16	.18	.21	.12	—	.32	.34
E II	.26	.43	.30	.22	.08	.35	.38	.11	—	.36	.45
F I	.32	.50	.41	.36	.09	.19	.42	.01	.32	—	.28
F II	.51	.42	.43	.45	.24	.31	.47	.20	.36	—	.49
Comp. I	.06	.32	.46	.36	.30	.21	.45	.20	.34	.28	—
Comp. II	.12	.36	.48	.41	.31	.30	.51	.24	.45	.49	—

I = Initial Testing; II = Final Testing; N.D. = Nelson-Denny Reading Test

* The correlation between school marks and the other scores except Composites I and II is based on class E_1 only, N = 25; 127 cases were used in computing the correlation between school grades and the composite scores and the composite scores on the critical thinking tests.

TABLE 14

CORRELATION BETWEEN INITIAL AND RETEST SCORES
ON TESTS WHICH WERE ADMINISTERED TWICE

Test	CORRELATION BETWEEN TEST AND RETEST*	
	Class E1; N = 25	Class C5; N = 32
Otis I. Q.	.833	.798
A (Att.)	.810	.758
A (Cons.)	.480	.596
B–AR	.481	.500
C	.828	.661
D	.327	.274
E	.341	.631
F	.575	.748
Compos.	.629†	

* The above coefficients of correlation were computed for only two classes, one experimental and one control, to approximate the relationship between the test and retest Z-scores.   The critical thinking tests administered in September, 1938, were the first edition of the Watson-Glaser Tests of Critical Thinking.   The retests administered in December, 1938, were a revision of the initial tests.   The revision consisted chiefly in the refinement of language used in the test items in order to eliminate possible ambiguity in some instances, and in the elimination of the least discriminating items and the substitution of new ones in their place.   In the second edition Tests C and D were divided into two parts, the first part not dealing at all with controversial socio-economic-political issues, and the second part dealing only with such issues.

† The correlation between Compos. I and Compos. II was obtained for the entire experimental group, N = 127.

The low correlation (.06 on the initial test and .12 on the retest) between the average of school marks for the preceding year and the total composite score on the critical thinking tests, is interesting to note. *A priori,* one might expect that pupils who manifest superior ability in perceiving correctly the kinds of relationships involved in the test items would manifest superior ability in "seeing into" problems involved in their studies, and thus obtain relatively high marks. It may well be that correlations between school marks and composite critical thinking score would vary greatly among different schools employing different bases for judging scholastic achievement. It may also be that the correlation found between those two variables for the group measured is not closely representative of the degree of relationship which obtains among the total population in the two schools from which the sample was drawn. The coefficient, like all statistical numbers, is subject to fluctuations of sampling. The question of representativeness of sampling might, of course, be raised in connection with all the measures obtained. In view of the known circumstances related to the selection of these experimental classes, however, there is reason to believe that the sample was approximately representative.

Scores obtained on Test C, the Inference Test, correlate higher with the Otis intelligence test and the Nelson-Denny reading test than do scores obtained on any other of the critical thinking tests. The correlation coefficient was found to be .52 between Otis and Inference, and .55 between Nelson-Denny and Inference on the initial testing. Otis and Nelson-Denny scores were found to correlate .69 with each other. The relationship among those three tests indicates that to a considerable extent they measure a similar ability, or group of abilities, but they also measure abilities which are different from any factors or abilities which are measured in common by the three tests. Although in general students who made a high score on the Otis test tended also to make a high score on the Nelson-Denny and on the Inference Test, nevertheless there were many individual exceptions to this general group tendency.[4]

Scores obtained on Test D, the Generalization Test, correlate lower with the Otis Intelligence Test than do scores obtained on any other of the critical thinking tests, and show a slight negative correlation with Nelson-Denny reading scores (−.06). Teachers report that it is relatively easy to get students to appreciate something of the faulty reasoning involved in overgeneralizations.

The intercorrelations among the tests of critical thinking

---

[4] Statistical numbers supply in a condensed way information about the characteristics of a group. They do not supply information about any *one* individual in a group unless it is known that all the individuals are the same with reference to the characteristics measured or unless we find a perfect positive or a perfect negative correlation (+ 1.00 or − 1.00). This elementary fact is sometimes overlooked in making inferences from statistical measures.

all are positive but low, the highest being between the Inference and Evaluation of Arguments Tests which was found to be .42 on the initial testing. This supports the opinion that the tests are measuring different, though interrelated abilities. The low correlations between each of the individual critical thinking tests and the composite Z-score sum of the remaining tests is further evidence that the tests are measuring different abilities.[5]

A positive correlation was found between each of the critical thinking tests and scores on the Otis Intelligence Test, ranging from .03 for the Generalization Test to .52 for the Inference Test on the initial testing. The composite Z-scores obtained on the battery of critical thinking tests was found to correlate .46 with the intelligence test scores, indicating that while the Otis and the Watson-Glaser tests measure some overlapping abilities, they also measure definitely different abilities. This finding supports the assumption stated in Chapter I of this study that the abilities involved in critical thinking are related to, yet considerably different from, the abilities measured by commonly used intelligence tests.

Data in Table 14 indicate that as a group the pupils tended to stand in a more or less similar relative relationship with regard to scores on the critical thinking tests after a ten-week interval, although there were many individual shifts in score and in relative ranking. The test-retest correlation on the total battery of critical thinking tests for the experimental pupils, with special instruction intervening, was found to be .63. It is difficult to account for a test-retest correlation as low as .27 for a control class unless some of the students "learned the answers" to that test (D) between test and

[5] It should be noted, however, that all the subjects to whom the tests were administered were twelfth grade pupils. The range of talent was therefore restricted; the group was relatively homogeneous. The coefficient of correlation r between the separate tests in the Watson-Glaser battery would be considerably higher if a more variable group—say a representative sample of cases from all grades in high school and college—were tested. All the correlations reported in Table 13, then, are lower than would be found if the tests were given to a more heterogeneous group in which there was a wide range of talent.

retest while others did not, or unless they did a great deal of "guessing" at answers, thus making for unreliability.

Factors Related to the Development of Critical Thinking

What characteristics, if any, distinguish between those who scored high and those who scored low on the initial administration of the critical thinking tests? What characteristics distinguish those in the experimental group who gained the most and those who gained the least after special instruction? Tables 15, 15A, and 16 present data pertinent to these questions.

Column A indicates the initial test mean (or percentage) for all the pupils both in the experimental and control group on each of the factors tested.

Column B of Table 15 indicates the mean score on each of the factors numbered from 1 to 17, obtained by those whose composite critical thinking scores fell in the top 27 per cent of the distribution of total composite scores on the critical thinking tests. For example, those in the top 27 per cent of the distribution of critical thinking scores had a mean age of 15.90 years. The percentage entries in Table 15A for factors 18 to 26 are read as follows: Among those in the top 27 per cent of the critical thinking distribution, 84 per cent answered *yes* to the question on Part V of the Maller-Glaser Interest-Values Inventory, "Do you feel that your good qualities are generally appreciated and recognized by your family?" Column C is read in the same manner as Column B, but refers to those in the top 10 per cent of the critical thinking distribution. Columns D and E refer to those in the bottom 27 per cent and the bottom 10 per cent of the critical thinking distribution.

Column F indicates the difference in mean scores on each of the factors from 1 to 17 (Table 15), or the difference in percentage answering *yes* to items 18 to 26 (Table 15A), between those in the top 27 per cent and those in the bottom 27 per cent of the critical thinking distribution. Column G indicates the difference in score between the top and bottom 10 per cent. In general, if a factor is related to the develop-

TABLE 15

MEANS ON ALL TESTS OF THOSE WHO SCORED HIGH AND THOSE WHO SCORED LOW
ON THE INITIAL CRITICAL THINKING TESTS

Factor		A	B	C	D	E	F	G
		All Cases N = 259	27% Initially Highest Compos. I	10% Initially Highest Compos. I	27% Initially Lowest Compos. I	10% Initially Lowest Compos. I	B–D	C–E
1. Age	Mean	16.49	15.90	15.95	16.68	16.67	− .78	− .73
	S. D.	9.85						
2. School Marks	Mean	74.80	78.67	79.95	72.85	71.80	5.82	8.15
	S. D.	5.92						
3. Home	Mean	52.00	55.40	54.20	51.01	52.46	4.39	1.74
	S. D.	12.62						
4. T Value	Mean	19.74	20.01	20.62	18.85	19.70	1.16	.92
	S. D.	5.91						
5. A Value	Mean	16.62	17.51	15.38	15.43	14.70	2.08	.68
	S. D.	6.49						
6. S Value	Mean	18.58	18.38	18.38	18.51	18.19	− .13	.19
	S. D.	5.14						
7. E Value	Mean	20.88	20.00	21.85	23.06	23.41	− 3.06	− 1.56
	S .D.	6.82						
8. Emot. Satis.	Mean	69.20	69.65	73.27	69.13	72.11	.52	1.16
	S. D.	16.00						
9. N. D. Read. Perc. R.	Mean	57.22	70.47	77.08	45.85	39.77	24.62	37.31
	S. D.	24.34						
10. Otis I. Q.	Mean	106.77	112.96	114.23	101.25	96.37	11.71	17.86
	S. D.	10.27						
11. A. Att.	Mean	67.49	72.29	74.92	63.32	60.52	8.97	14.40
	S. D.	10.05						
12. A. Cons.	Mean	85.20	56.69	55.54	39.96	29.00	16.73	26.54
	S. D.	8.15						
13. B–AR	Mean	57.80	58.68	66.65	43.77	42.45	14.91	24.20
	S. D.	13.83						
14. C	Mean	56.44	59.82	63.73	39.10	31.81	20.72	31.92
	S. D.	10.90						
15. D	Mean	58.47	58.26	61.69	40.72	37.19	17.54	24.50
	S. D.	10.61						
16. E	Mean	63.90	60.51	64.38	39.51	34.15	21.00	30.23
	S. D.	9.56						
17. F	Mean	33.20	61.10	71.88	39.66	39.00	21.44	32.88
	S. D.	19.02						
Compos. Cr. Th. Score	Mean	299.05	357.68	387.58	209.58	242.65	148.10	144.93
	S. D.	50.38						

TABLE 15A

Factor	A	B	C	D	E	F	G
	All Cases N = 259	27% Initially Highest Compos. I	10% Initially Highest Compos. I	27% Initially Lowest Compos. I	10% Initially Lowest Compos. I	B–D	C–E
18. Regarded self religious	38	25	4	45	41	− 20	− 37
19. Regarded self appreciated by family	84	84	85	85	81	− 1	4
20. Regarded self appreciated at school	71	81	81	62	70	19	11
21. Regarded self appreciated by friends	86	86	85	82	85	4	0
22. Had opportunity to attain ambition	48	38	41	54	41	− 16	0
23. Had feeling of success in studies	69	70	85	76	85	− 6	0
24. Had satisfactory sex adjustment	74	70	67	73	74	− 3	− 7
25. Had satisfying friendships	87	88	78	87	93	1	− 15
26. Had opportunity to express self	65	67	78	49	58	18	19

ment of critical thinking, then the difference between the 10 per cent extremes should be greater than between the top and bottom 27 per cent.

Since all the students involved in this study were in the beginning of the fourth year of high school, the range of ages is restricted. Within this range, age was not found to be related to the development of critical thinking; age did not sharply distinguish those who made low scores from those who made high scores on the critical thinking tests. Those who made the highest initial critical thinking scores were younger than those who made the lowest scores, but the younger pupils in the same grade as older pupils are likely to be the brighter pupils, so that their higher scores on the critical thinking tests probably is a function of superior intelligence.

School marks were found to be related to scores on the critical thinking tests. The average school grades for the preceding year of the top 27 per cent of the distribution were 5.82 points higher than those in the bottom 27 per cent of the distribution. This difference is equal to almost one standard deviation of the distribution. Between the top and bottom 10 per cent the difference in grades was found to be 8.15.

A slight tendency was found for those pupils from homes with a higher rating on socio-economic status to do better on the critical thinking tests than those pupils from homes with a lower rating on socio-economic status. But the difference was not found to grow progressively. Those in the upper 27 per cent of the distribution had a home rating of 4.39 points higher than those in the bottom 27 per cent of the critical thinking distribution, while the difference among the 10 per cent extremes was only 1.74 points. Since the standard deviation of the home rating distribution was found to be 12.62, the differences noted are negligible.

Scores on the Interest-Values Inventory were not found to be appreciably related to scores on the critical thinking tests, although there was a tendency for pupils with a dominant economic-interest value to score lower on the critical thinking tests than pupils dominant in either the theoretic, aesthetic, or social-interest values.

The emotional satisfaction score obtained from Part V of the Interest-Values Inventory was not found to be related to scores on the critical thinking tests. There was a tendency, however, for those who answered *yes* to the question, "Do you regard yourself as a religious person?" to score lower on the critical thinking tests than those who answered *no*.

The two factors most clearly related to scores on the critical thinking tests were found to be scores on the Otis intelligence test and the Nelson-Denny reading tests. A difference of 11.71 I. Q. points was found between the means of those in the top and those in the bottom 27 per cent of the critical thinking distribution, and a difference of 17.86 I. Q. points was found between the means of the top and bottom 10 per cent on the Otis test. The latter difference represents almost two standard deviations on the total distribution of Otis scores. The top and bottom 27 per cent difference on the Nelson-Denny test was found to be 24.62 percentiles, or a difference of about one standard deviation.

Table 16 presents data pertinent to the second question, posed under the heading "Factors Related to the Development of Critical Thinking," "What characteristics, if any, distinguish between those who gained the most and those who gained the least after the special instruction?"

The change in attitude score on Test A, A Survey of Opinions, apparently was not related to the amount of gain in critical thinking score between initial test and retest. The views these pupils held with regard to certain socio-economic questions were not found to be related to whether they *gained* much or little on the critical thinking tests, although a correlation of .29 was found between a tendency in favor of the "progressive" position (as defined in Test A) and initial composite score on the critical thinking tests.

Those who gained most in total composite score gained more on each test in the critical thinking battery than did those who gained least in composite score. Since gains in

TABLE 16

CHANGES BETWEEN INITIAL AND RETEST SCORES OF THOSE IN EXPERIMENTAL GROUP
WHO GAINED MOST AND THOSE WHO GAINED LEAST

Test	B* Mean Gain of 27% Who Gained Most in Compos. Score	C Mean Gain of 10% Who Gained Most in Compos. Score	D Mean Gain (or Loss) of 27% Who Gained Least in Compos. Score	E Mean Gain (or Loss) of 10% Who Gained Least in Compos. Score	F B–D	G C–E
1. Otis Intell.	4.09	4.46	3.63	4.15	.46	.31
2. A (Att.)	3.97	2.77	4.00	1.54	− .03	1.23
3. A (Cons.)	13.40	17.54	− 6.34	− 9.62	19.74	27.16
4. B–AR	25.03	29.92	13.57	19.85	11.46	10.07
5. C	14.03	10.92	4.71	2.15	9.32	8.77
6. D	27.37	32.23	2.00	− 7.31	25.37	39.54
7. E	17.34	23.23	2.54	− 2.23	14.80	25.46
8. F	21.03	25.69	7.80	5.00	13.23	20.69
9. Compos.	119.11	139.54	23.89	7.46	95.22	132.08

* Since there were 127 pupils in the experimental group, 27 per cent represents 34 pupils, and 10 per cent, 13 pupils.

composite score are made up of gains on each of the tests contributing to the composite, this result is to be expected. The important question is on *which* tests were the differences in gain greatest and on which least. The difference in gain on Test D, the Generalization Test, between those in the top 10 per cent and the bottom 10 per cent of the distribution of gains in total composite critical thinking score, was found to be 39.54 points. This gain is more than three times the standard deviation of 10.61 obtained for the entire distribution of scores on Test D (see Table 15). The difference between the top and bottom 27 per cent groups was 25.37

points. It has previously been noted that the ability measured by the Generalization Test is one of the abilities involved in critical thinking which is most readily susceptible to improvement upon instruction. Gains on this test then, contributed a good deal to the total amount of gain made by the groups which gained the most.

Second to the Generalization Test, the consistency score on Test A, the Survey of Opinions Test, distinguished most sharply between those who gained most and least in component critical thinking score. The difference in gain on Test A (Consistency) between the top and bottom 27 per cent groups was 19.74 points, and 27.16 points for the top and bottom 10 per cent groups, with a standard deviation of 8.15 for the total number of cases.

Test C, the Inference Test, was the least discriminating among the extremes of the distributions, as would be expected from the previous data on comparison of mean gains.

Relationship between Intelligence and Gain on the Critical Thinking Tests after Special Instruction

Data in Table 16 indicate that pupils in the group which gained the most and pupils in the group which gained the least between initial and retest composite critical thinking score differed very little in the amount they gained in I. Q. points on the Otis intelligence test. But what was the mean intelligence quotient of those in the experimental group who gained the most on the critical thinking tests as compared with those who gained the least? Is it essential to have a relatively high I. Q. in order to profit from training in critical thinking? Data in Tables 17, 18, 19 furnish answers to these questions.

The coefficient of correlation between *gains* on the critical thinking tests and initial scores on the Otis test was found to be .334 for the experimental group. It is important to note that while those who gained most in composite critical thinking score had as a group a slightly higher I. Q. than those who gained least (Table 17); nevertheless, many pupils who gained most had relatively low I. Q.'s. Among the thirty-five

TABLE 17

INTELLIGENCE QUOTIENTS OF THOSE WHO GAINED MOST AND LEAST IN CRITICAL
THINKING TESTS IN THE EXPERIMENTAL GROUP

Distribution of Gains in Composite Scores	No.	Mean I. Q.	Range of I. Q.'s
Top 10%	13	106.38	95–122
Top 27%	35	106.80	92–122
Bottom 27%	35	105.40	86–129
Bottom 10%	13	104.77	86–112

Mean I. Q. for E group = 106.60 (N = 127)
Mean I. Q. for all subjects = 106.77 (N = 259)

TABLE 18

DISTRIBUTION OF INTELLIGENCE TEST QUOTIENTS OF 27 PER CENT WHO GAINED
MOST IN CRITICAL THINKING

I. Q.	Frequency
120–124.9	2
115–119.9	8
110–114.9	3
105–109.9	8
100–104.9	6
95– 99.9	6
90– 94.9	2
(N = 35*)	

* Twenty-seven per cent of 127 is 34, but two persons gained the same number of
points which marked off the top 27 per cent; the two cases were therefore included
instead of only one.

cases in the top 27 per cent of gains in composite critical
thinking score, twenty-two pupils or 63 per cent of the group
had I. Q.'s of less than 110, and 23 per cent had I. Q.'s of
less than 100 (Table 18).

It may be noted (Table 19) that those in the top 27 per
cent of the I. Q. distribution obtained an initial mean score of
321.14 on the critical thinking tests, while those in the bottom
27 per cent of the I. Q. distribution obtained an initial mean
score of 277.19—a difference of 43.95 Z-score points. This

TABLE 19

GAINS IN CRITICAL THINKING SCORE OF THOSE IN THE TOP AND THOSE IN THE BOTTOM
27 PER CENT IN THE DISTRIBUTION OF I. Q.'s
(Experimental Group, N = 127)

Distribution of I. Q.'s in Initial Testing	Initial Mean Compos. Crit. Thinking Score	Retest Mean Compos. Crit. Thinking Score	Gain in Crit. Thinking Score between Initial Test and Retest	Range of Gains
Top 10% (Mean I. Q. = 123.47)	344.67	421.60	76.93	24–131
Top 27% (Mean I. Q. = 118.31)	321.14	400.72	79.58	11–145
Bottom 27% (Mean I. Q. = 95.94)	277.19	347.78	70.58	6–163
Bottom 10% (Mean I. Q. = 91.00)	252.92	335.46	82.54	15–163

checks with the correlation (Table 13) of .46 between the Otis intelligence test and the critical thinking battery. Note, however, that the mean *gain* of those in the top 27 per cent was only 9 Z-score points more than the mean gain of those in the bottom 27 per cent. And when we compare the gains (on the critical thinking tests) of those in the top and bottom 10 per cent of the I. Q. distribution, we find that those with the very lowest I. Q.'s gained 5.61 Z-score points more than those with the very highest I. Q.'s.

At first thought this latter finding may appear to be at variance with the finding of a positive correlation of .33 between intelligence and gains in critical thinking. It is not a contradiction, however, since the correlation holds for the entire group (N=127), whereas this reversal of the group trend applies only to the top and bottom 10 per cent of the cases.

Relationships between Initial Scores on the Critical Thinking Battery, and Retest Gains

There is evidence presented in Table 20 that those who gained most made, as a group, an initially lower mean composite score than those who gained least.

TABLE 20

CRITICAL THINKING SCORES OF THOSE WHO GAINED MOST AND LEAST AFTER TRAINING

	A Initial Mean	Initial Range	B Retest Mean	Retest Range	Difference B − A
Top 27% who gained most in composite score	284.51	171–396	387.93	281–489	103.42
Bottom 27% who gained least in composite critical thinking score	302.32	213–425	311.23	187–444	8.91
Difference in mean score between top and bottom 27%	17.81		76.70		94.51

It will be noted that the pupils in the group which gained the most in composite critical thinking score made an initial mean score of 284.51, whereas the group which gained least made an initial mean score of 302.32—a difference of 17.81 points in favor of the group which gained least. Thus, while the mean gain of those pupils who gained most was 103.42 points, as compared with a mean gain of only 8.91 points for the pupils who gained least, the pupils in the top 27 per cent had "farther to go," since they started from a mean which was 17.81 points below the mean of the other group. This confirms Hill's [128] findings that low initial scores tend to be accompanied by high gains. Pupils who made relatively high scores on the initial testing manifested relatively good ability to think critically before the special training. Another factor which probably is involved here, however, is the fact that the ceiling on some of the tests, such as the Generalization Test, may be too low for persons who have grasped fairly well the concepts involved in the items presented in that test. A low ceiling on a test would serve to limit gains of persons who score high initially. In general, however, the ceiling on the tests is much higher than the level of competence in ability to think critically of all but very exceptional students. The highest possible score in raw score points on the battery used in this study is 600 points; the highest initial score obtained by any student was 444 raw score points.

*Relationships between Answers to Questions Bearing
on "Happiness" or Emotional Satisfaction, and
Gain in Critical Thinking Score*

A tabulation was made of the answers to Part V of the
Interest-Values Inventory by the pupils in the top and in the
bottom 27 per cent of the distribution of gains in total component critical thinking score. The results of this tabulation
are presented in Table 21.

TABLE 21

EXPRESSIONS OF FEELINGS OF SATISFACTION AND DISSATISFACTION OF THOSE WHO
GAINED MOST AND LEAST IN CRITICAL THINKING SCORE

Question	A Per Cent Among Highest 27% Answering Yes	B Per Cent Among Highest 10% Answering Yes	C Per Cent Among Lowest 27% Answering Yes	D Per Cent Among Lowest 10% Answering Yes	A − C	B − D
Regards self as religious	39	25	42	46	−3	−21
Feels appreciated by family	67	75	86	92	−19	−17
Feels appreciated at school	67	50	81	77	−14	−27
Feels appreciated among friends	81	75	89	85	−8	−10
Has opportunity to attain ambition	39	25	44	38	−5	−13
Feels successful at studies	72	75	69	85	3	−10
Feels satisfactory adjustment to opposite sex	67	67	89	92	−22	−25
Has satisfying friendships	81	75	94	100	−13	−25
Has opportunity to express self	47	25	53	46	−6	−21

Fewer pupils among the 10 per cent who gained most than
among the 10 per cent who gained least answered *yes* to the
question: "Do you regard yourself a religious person?" The
difference may be due largely to a chance fluctuation on sam-

pling, however, since the top and bottom 27 per cent groups were not appreciably distinguished by this item.

The tabulation of answers to the questions in Part V of the Interest-Values Inventory reveals that in every instance except in answering the question "Do you feel that you are making a success of your studies?" more pupils in the bottom 27 per cent of the distribution of gains in composite critical thinking score answered *yes* than in the top 27 per cent of the distribution. This finding may perhaps be explained on the ground that the pupils who gained the most in critical thinking score were, as a group, also found to be intellectually superior to those who gained least. Persons who possess a combination of relatively high mentality and manifest a readiness to respond to training in critical thinking may well be expected to possess greater sensitivities, subtler and more varied personality needs, a sharper awareness of the nature of their dissatisfactions, and more resistance to saying *yes* than persons who possess a relatively low mental level and lack readiness to respond to instruction in critical thinking. Those who gained most, then, probably are not as easily "satisfied" as those who gained least.

Another factor to be considered is that those who manifest a readiness to respond to training in critical thinking may be more honest in admitting such things as a feeling of unsatisfactory adjustment to members of the opposite sex, or a feeling that their good qualities are not generally appreciated by their families or by their teachers, while those who do not manifest a readiness to respond to training in critical thinking may be more likely to "try to make a good impression" in answering the questionnaire.

Comparison of Difficulty of Test Items Bearing
on Socio-Economic Issues with Test Items
Bearing on Non-Socio-Economic Issues

Another matter of interest in connection with the test results is a comparison of scores on Parts I and II of Tests C and D. Both of these tests contain the same number of items in Parts I and II. The content of the items in Part I, however, deals with relatively abstract questions while the content of the items in Part II deals with controversial socio-economic and political issues. From the point of view of the logic involved, both parts are of equal difficulty. Test results show, therefore, whether pupils tend to make more logical errors in responding to items which deal with issues concerning which they are likely to have strong feelings than they make in responding to relatively abstract items. Table 22 shows the scores obtained on the separate parts of Tests C and D by both the experimental and control classes in December, 1938.

TABLE 22

SCORES BETWEEN PARTS I (ABSTRACT) AND II (CONTROVERSIAL)
ON TESTS C AND D

| Class | Mean Test C | | Diff. | Mean Test D | | Diff. |
	Part I	Part II	M–M	Part I	Part II	M–M
E1	32.64	30.00	2.64	34.14	28.14	6.00
E2	35.38	31.72	3.66	36.47	32.24	4.23
E3	35.56	33.56	2.00	38.42	33.52	4.90
E4	33.80	29.76	4.04	39.66	33.54	6.12
Compos. E	34.38	31.21	3.17	37.53	32.18	5.35
C1	35.13	30.80	4.33	35.66	29.33	6.33
C2	32.47	30.03	2.44	35.58	33.08	2.50
C3	32.76	29.35	3.41	36.65	31.73	4.92
C4	30.34	26.80	3.54	32.50	29.79	2.71
Compos. C	32.59	29.16	3.43	35.08	30.98	4.10

Each of the eight classes to which the tests were given made a lower mean score on the part which deals with controversial socio-economic and political issues than they made on the part dealing with relatively abstract questions. This finding supports the hypothesis that pupils tend to make more logical errors in responding to items which deal with issues concerning which they are likely to have strong feelings than they make in responding to relatively abstract items. Another possible factor contributing to this difference in mean score on the two parts, however, is the language in Part II of Tests C and D which is somewhat more difficult than in Part I, because of the nature of the content of the socio-economic problems.

Sex Differences

The scores of boys and girls were separated on all tests, and separate means were computed. No significant difference was found between boys and girls on any of the test scores.

EVALUATION BY RETESTING AFTER A SIX-MONTH INTERVAL

At the end of May, 1939, a postcard was sent to each student who had participated in the experiment as a member of one of the experimental classes, asking his cooperation in meeting at some convenient time for the purpose of again taking some of the critical thinking tests.

Forty pupils, twenty-one boys and nineteen girls, made and kept appointments for retesting. Eleven of the students were from class E1, twelve from class E2, eight from class E3, and nine from class E4. The results of this retest are presented in Table 23.

TABLE 23

SCORES OF FORTY PUPILS RETESTED SIX MONTHS AFTER CONCLUSION OF SPECIAL WORK IN CRITICAL THINKING

Test	DECEMBER 1938			MAY 1939			Change
	Range	Mean	S. D.	Range	Mean	S. D.	
I. Q.	89–142	111.20	10.52				
B–AR	64–100	78.70	10.79	52–100	75.70	12.69	−3.00
C	48–88	67.50	9.28	48–86	68.30	9.03	+ .80
D	50–88	68.95	9.74	55–100	75.25	12.01	+6.30
Compos.	278–502	377.70	52.60				

Since the students had to meet the tester either during their free periods or after school hours, it was important that the testing time be reduced to a minimum. Tests B–AR, C, and D were selected for retesting.

The mean I. Q. of the students who responded to the request for an appointment for retesting in May, 1939, was 111.20 on the retest, whereas the mean I. Q. of the entire experimental group on the retest in December, 1938, was 109.66. The forty pupils who took the follow-up test were a little higher in mental ability as a group than the entire experimental group. Similarly, the composite retest mean score of the entire experimental group was 370.15 (see Table 3, page 132), whereas the composite retest mean score of these forty pupils was 377.70. While one cannot be sure that the factors which contributed to making these particular forty students willing and able to give up their own time for follow-up testing do not affect their value as a sample, their test scores would indicate that they were but slightly superior to the entire experimental group. Assuming that the follow-up scores made by these forty students are nearly representative of the follow-up scores of the entire group, and that scores on Tests B–AR, C, and D furnish a fair estimate of retention of ability to respond properly to the problems in the critical thinking tests, then there is evidence that the understanding the students acquired tends to be relatively stable after six months. There was an average loss of three points on Test B–AR, a gain of .80 on Test C, and a gain of 6.30 on Test D. There is a possibility that a few of the students might have learned that the response "DK" (Don't know how many) was scored as the best answer to all items on Test D; if so, the further gain of 6.30 points could perhaps be accounted for.

AN EXPERIMENT WITH THE LESSON UNITS WITH A TENTH GRADE CLASS

At the same time that the main experiment with the four twelfth grade experimental and four twelfth grade control classes was undertaken, the lesson units were also tried with one tenth grade class, E5. Another tenth grade in the same school (in New York City), designated as C5, was used as a control group. Data concerning the two classes are given in Table 24.

TABLE 24

TENTH GRADE EXPERIMENTAL AND CONTROL CLASSES

Group	Factor	Range	Mean	S. D.
E5*	Age	12–8 to 16–6	14.51 yrs.	11.83 mos.
C5†	Age	12–4 to 15–4	14.03 yrs.	11.16 mos.
E5	Av. Sch. Gr. Prec. Yr.	64–93.4	80.32	70.84
C5	Av. Sch. Gr. Prec. Yr.	65.6–89.0	80.24	−14.43
E5	Otis I. Q.	97–126	112.61	8.04
C5	Otis I. Q.	92–128	113.16	8.84
E5	Nelson-Denny Read. Percentile Rank	26–98	69.63	20.78
C5	Nelson-Denny Read. Percentile Rank	60–99	81.91	10.17

* N = 41   † N = 32

While these tenth grade pupils were on the average more than two years younger than the twelfth grade pupils who participated in the main experiment, their I. Q.'s and previous average school marks were higher. Table 25 shows the test-retest scores of groups E5 and C5 on the critical thinking tests.

A comparison of the test-retest results between these two tenth grade classes and the four twelfth grade experimental and four control classes (see Tables 3–11) reveals that the twelfth grade experimental classes gained more from the instruction, as measured by the tests, than the tenth grade class. Whereas the 127 twelfth grade pupils in the experimental group gained on the average 71.08 points in composite score on the retest, and 30.16 points more than their controls gained, the forty-one pupils in this tenth grade experimental group gained 57.78 points in composite score on the retest, and 20.12 points more than their controls gained.

The gain of the experimental tenth grade pupils over the control tenth grade pupils is significant, although not as marked as with the twelfth grade pupils. It might be noted here that the teacher of the tenth grade experimental class deviated more from the suggested presentation in the lesson

TABLE 25
Tenth-Grade Test-Retest Scores

Group	Test	Initial Test			Retest			Change
		Range	Mean	S. D.	Range	Mean	S. D.	
E5	A(Att.)	51– 87	69.27	7.83	52– 92	69.03	10.58	— .24
C5	A(Att.)	54– 82	69.63	6.46	43– 83	68.06	8.32	—1.57
E5	A(Cons.)	72–100	85.66	7.00	72–100	90.64	7.03	4.98
C5	A(Cons.)	74– 99	87.75	5.62	72–100	88.25	8.00	.50
E5	B–AR	32– 88	55.81	16.64	44– 96	72.59	14.03	16.78
C5	B–AR	24– 88	55.70	14.96	40– 96	68.75	13.98	13.00
E5	C	36– 72	59.88	8.62	48– 78	65.17	8.04	9.29
C5	C	38– 72	57.13	6.63	48– 74	61.38	7.13	4.25
E5	D	42– 90	66.05	9.85	55–100	75.50	10.31	9.45
C5	D	43– 90	67.75	9.85	47.5– 92	69.58	12.09	1.83
E5	E	47.5–85	65.67	8.47	42.5– 85	68.44	9.13	3.17
C5	E	50– 85	65.92	7.12	57.5– 90	71.01	7.23	5.09
E5	F	2– 79	32.51	20.44	0– 87	44.78	24.00	12.27
C5	F	4– 74	27.41	18.91	3– 75	37.31	20.32	9.90
E5	Compos.	255–401	315.71	40.50	266–470	373.49	41.38	57.78
C5	Compos.	233–387	314.28	42.24	281–426	351.94	46.61	37.66

units than any of the four twelfth grade teachers. It is not possible to determine whether the change in the content of instruction affected the amount of gain on the critical thinking tests, and, if it did, whether it made for more or less gain. Another factor which may well be pertinent to the comparison of these two tenth grade classes is the fact that the control class was considerably better in reading ability than the experimental class. The mean percentage rank of the control class on the Nelson-Denny Reading test was 81.91 as compared with 69.63 for the experimental class.

The tenth grade experimental group gained more in comparison with the tenth grade control group on the Inference and Generalization Tests than did the twelfth grade group in comparison with its control, while the twelfth grade group gained more in comparison with its control in attitude score on the Survey of Opinions Test and on the Logical Reasoning, Discrimination of Arguments, and Evaluation of Arguments Tests than the tenth grade class.

A SPECIAL INVESTIGATION OF THE RELATIONSHIP BETWEEN "CRITICAL THINKING" AND "CRITICAL READING"

During the period of work with the special lesson units the author frequently visited the four experimental classes. On the basis of (1) observations during these visits, (2) study of data obtained from the tests (such as the correlation coefficient of .47 between reading test scores and average school marks), (3) interviews with some of the students, including analysis of their reasoning processes in answering as they did on certain test items, and (4) study of some of the literature and experimental findings in the field of remedial reading, there seemed reasonable grounds for believing that ability to comprehend and use language with clarity, accuracy, and discrimination probably was the most important component in the second and third aspects of critical thinking, as critical thinking is defined in this study.[6]

There is abundant evidence that reading, language, and thinking are intimately related.[7] Many persons who graduate even from our high schools are seriously deficient in reading comprehension although they know how to read in the mechanical sense of being able to read words in print. A fundamental assumption in this study, implied in Chapter I in connection with the discussion of the necessity for a democratic state to train its citizens to think critically, is that it is highly important for the large majority of the population to be able to read thoughtfully and critically and weigh the

---

[6] Critical thinking . . . involves . . . (1) an attitude of being disposed to consider in a thoughtful way the problems and subjects that come within the range of one's experience, (2) knowledge of the methods of logical inquiry and reasoning, and (3) some skill in applying these methods.

[7] The evidence for the relationship between reading, language, and thinking is especially well presented in *Reading in General Education*, American Council on Education, Washington, D. C., 1940.

evidence that is presented to them. Traxler presents this view:

If the need (for a program of remedial reading throughout the secondary schools of America) is met, teachers of remedial reading will not be satisfied with the mere mechanical aspects of the reading process which so often engage the greater share of attention in contemporary programs of this kind. They will recognize that, while several other aspects are important in a remedial reading program, the most significant phase of the work is the . . . training in the tools and methods of thinking. . . . Any conception of reading is inadequate that fails to include reflection, critical evaluation, and clarification of meaning. . . . Maturity of reading is essentially maturity of thinking, and . . . every time a child is given a new concept—one that is really his—and every time he is enabled to see a new relationship between ideas—one that he truly apprehends—he has been brought a little distance along the road toward independent and efficient use of man's most important tool.[8]

Unfortunately, the author did not fully appreciate the relationship between reading ability and ability to think critically when he began this study. Consequently, the test of reading ability was administered only once—with the general retesting at the end of the experiment. Since the special work with the lesson units in critical thinking was again undertaken in the Newark school (by the same two teachers but with different classes) at the beginning of the semester following the conclusion of the experiment, it was possible to explore further the relationship between critical thinking and the kind of critical reading Traxler has described. Accordingly, as a separate experiment, both the Martin Reading Comprehension Test [9] and the Watson-Glaser tests were administered to an average

---

[8] A. E. Traxler, "Problems of Group Remedial Reading in the Secondary School," *High Points*, Vol. XX, pp. 5–18, 1938.

[9] The Martin Reading Comprehension Test is a new diagnostic reading test for use at the secondary and college levels. While this test does not attempt to measure all of the abilities involved in critical reading, it appears to be a more satisfactory instrument for measuring certain important aspects of critical reading than are other reading tests available at the time of this writing (1940). The experimental form of the test may be obtained from Dr. Margaret E. Martin, Teachers College, Columbia University. The Introduction to the test may be found in the Supplement to Lesson Unit 2, Generalization and Probable Inference.

and a superior twelfth grade English class [10] in the spring semester of 1939. Since these two classes were studied to determine the relationship between the pupils' scores on the Martin Reading Comprehension Test and the Watson-Glaser Tests of Critical Thinking, the two classes were considered as one group for purposes of increasing facility in making the computations.

TABLE 26

DATA CONCERNING THE SPRING 1939 GROUP (N = 50)

Item	Initial Range	Initial Mean I	S. D.	Retest Range	Retest Mean II	S. D.	Diff. M_{II}– M_I
Age	14–6 to 19–8	16–4	1.19				
Otis I. Q.	89–133	107.90	12.15				
A (Cons.)	26– 98	83.26	13.42	44–100	87.06	11.38	3.80
B–AR	32– 88	61.20	13.88	40–100	76.56	13.13	15.36
C	32– 82	60.32	11.96	34– 88	67.00	9.77	6.68
D	16– 84	58.44	13.28	50– 97	71.39	12.13	12.95
E	48– 97	65.65	9.37	48– 88	71.14	9.67	5.49
F	4– 97	41.66	23.51	6– 96	51.28	26.38	9.62
Composite	128–435	313.56	69.84	154–490	376.88	77.44	63.32

While this section of the study is not particularly concerned with the amount of gain between test and retest, it nevertheless is interesting to note that this group gained 63.32 points (Table 26) in total composite critical thinking score as compared with a gain in composite score of 71.08 points which was made by the experimental group of the preceding semester (see Table 3, page 132).

The correlations between the total composite score on the

[10] An average class is composed of students who received a mark of between 75–84 in that subject at the end of the preceding semester. A superior class is composed of students who received a mark above 85 in that subject at the end of the preceding semester.

Martin test and the total composite score on each of the Watson-Glaser tests, is given in Table 27.[11]

TABLE 27

CORRELATIONS BETWEEN THE MARTIN READING COMPREHENSION TEST AND THE WATSON–GLASER TESTS OF CRITICAL THINKING

Martin Reading Comprehension Test with:	r
Watson-Glaser:	
Initial Composite	.769
Retest Composite	.816
A (Cons.)	.361
B–AR	.702
C	.743
D	.422
E	.491
F	.767

A fairly high correlation, .769, was found between initial composite scores on the critical thinking tests and total composite scores on what might be termed a "test of critical reading." This relationship went up to .816 when the retest scores on the critical thinking tests (after the pupils had had the special training in critical thinking) were correlated with the scores on the Martin test. Tests C and F in the critical thinking series have the highest correlation among the separate tests with the Nelson-Denny Reading Test (Table 13, page 143), they also have the highest correlation with the Martin test. But while Tests C and F were found to correlate respectively .55 and .50 with the Nelson-Denny test, they were found to correlate .74 and .77 with the Martin test. The Martin test probably could be used very successfully as material for classroom instruction and practice in trying to develop certain aspects of ability to think critically.

[11] The total composite score on the Martin test represents the sum of the Z-scores obtained on each of five of the sections contained in that test: (1) Main Points, (2) Specific Facts, (3) Cause and Effect, (4) Inferences, and (5) Vocabulary.

Data in Table 28 show the intercorrelations between the various sections of the Martin test, and their relationship to the Nelson-Denny test and the American Council Psychological Examination for high school students.

TABLE 28

INTERCORRELATIONS AMONG SECTIONS OF THE MARTIN TEST, AND THEIR RELATIONSHIP
TO THE NELSON–DENNY READING TEST AND AMERICAN
COUNCIL PSYCHOLOGICAL EXAMINATION

(N = 72 high school juniors)

	B	C	D	E	F	N–D Voc.	N–D Par.	N–D Tot.	A–C Psych. Exam.
Martin Section									
A*	.73	.55	.69	.68	.72	.59	.64	.762	.670
B		.84	.77	.87	.78	.67	.72	.748	.703
C			.67	.75	.73	.69	.66	.708	.691
D				.71	.94	.66	.74	.752	.652
E					.75	.71	.68	.859	.724
F						.77	.78	.812	.817
Martin Total								.842	.792
N–D Voc.							.74	.939	.752
N–D Par.								.899	.681
N–D Total									.782

* A = Main Points, B = Specific Facts, C = Organization of Specific Facts, D = Cause and Effect, E = Inferences, F = Vocabulary.

The intercorrelations among the sections of the Martin test are higher than the intercorrelations among the individual tests in the Watson-Glaser battery. Further work which has been done on the Martin test tends to show that these subtests are measuring highly related aspects of reading. Since this test was set up to approximate the natural study-type of reading situation as closely as possible, these high intercorrelations do not necessarily imply a criticism of the Martin battery. Furthermore, the fact that many of the questions on the Martin test were based upon the same reading passage probably raises the intercorrelation among these subtests. None of the individual tests in the Watson-Glaser battery, however, contain common materials.

There also appears to be a higher correlation between intelligence and the Martin test than between intelligence and the Watson-Glaser tests (see Table 13, page 143).

The data presented in the two preceding tables support the conclusion that the abilities measured by the Martin test of critical reading are highly correlated with the abilities measured by the tests of critical thinking. The ability to comprehend language with accuracy and discrimination is measured by both the Martin and the Watson-Glaser tests; the two tests, however, measure different as well as overlapping abilities. They may be considered supplementary to each other in the measurement of critical thinking. The author ventures the hypothesis that both tests are in turn highly correlated with some of the tests recently developed by the Evaluation in the Eight Year Study of the Progressive Education Association —notably their "Interpretation of Data" test.

The Retreat from Reason is the penalty we are paying for an inherent dichotomy in the way we educate people. The training of the statesman and the man of letters gives him no prevision of the technical forces which are shaping the society in which he lives. The education of the scientist and the technician leaves him indifferent to the social consequences of his own activities. Hence it is nobody's business to take stock of the resources of knowledge now available for social betterment. . . . If we are to arrest the Retreat from Reason, we have to devise an education . . . which will give us representatives who can cooperate intelligently with technical experts in constructive social enterprise.

—LANCELOT HOGBEN

CHAPTER V

Summary and Conclusions

SUMMARY

ONE hundred and fifty years of public education in the United States have resulted in a largely literate electorate. Our public education has not resulted, however, in the development of a sufficient proportion of citizens who can evaluate critically *what* they read, and who possess that degree of social understanding and critical-mindedness necessary to make intelligent judgments about public issues. Competent citizenship in a democracy calls for a good deal more than the ability to read and write. Among other things, it requires the ability to think critically.

While development of the ability to reason logically and think clearly for oneself has long been recognized by some educational leaders as a desirable and most important educational objective, our schools have not been adequately successful in their job of cultivating in pupils the ability to think critically about issues concerning which there is an honest (or even a dishonest) difference of opinion. Recently curriculum committees in several states and cities have urged renewed emphasis upon the development of critical thinking as one of the major objectives of education. By and large, however, our schools have not made a conscious and well-directed effort to realize this educational aim. By placing greater emphasis upon developing in pupils an attitude of wanting evidence as a basis for belief and upon guiding pupils in the processes and methods of arriving at well-founded answers rather than upon having pupils memorize accepted answers, our schools will be likely to succeed better in their objective of cultivating the spirit of inquiry and the ability to think critically.

Based upon the assumption that the ability to think critically, or at least important aspects of that ability as herein defined, can be improved by certain kinds of educational experiences in which the desired outcomes are set up as definite goals of instruction and the guiding principles and processes are made clear and usable to the learner, a series of eight lesson units was developed. These units are intended to make available materials and illustrative teaching procedures which may be used effectively by high school and college teachers, and, with modifications, by upper-grade elementary teachers as well, to stimulate growth in ability to think critically.

The content and procedures suggested in these lesson units were tried out experimentally with four twelfth grade English classes, each taught by a different teacher. Two of the classes were in a New York City high school, and two were in a high school in Newark, N. J. Four other English classes (in the same two schools), equated on certain background factors, such as grade in school and intelligence, were used as control groups. A battery of tests, including the Otis Quick-Scoring Mental Ability Test and the Watson-Glaser Tests of Critical Thinking, was administered to the experimental and control classes in September, 1938. The experimental classes then received for ten weeks the special instruction suggested in the lesson units. The control classes followed the usual course of study for twelfth grade English which in those schools included study of Macaulay's *Life of Johnson,* essays by Bacon, Morley, Addison, Steele, and Stevenson, a study of newspapers, and which included among its objectives the development of ability to think critically.

At the end of the ten-week period, the pupils in both the experimental and control classes were retested and their scores were analyzed. In addition, five other methods of evaluating the outcomes of instruction were employed. They were: (1) evaluation by the teachers of the experimental classes, (2) evaluation by pupils, (3) evaluation by interviews with selected students, (4) evaluation by the author as a classroom observer and from stenographic notes of classroom instruction, and (5) evaluation by retesting after a six-month interval.

After the conclusion of the experiment, the original eight lesson units were improved and revised.

CONCLUSIONS

1. The average gain (in composite Z-score) on the battery of critical thinking tests of the four experimental classes after ten weeks was significantly greater than the average gain of the four control classes on the same tests (diff./σ_d=6.09). This significant difference supports the conclusion that the lesson units which have been developed can be used effectively with high school (and probably college) students to stimulate growth in ability to think critically.

2. The improvement in ability to think critically appears to be somewhat general in character. There is evidence for some students of improvement in general disposition to consider problems thoughtfully, and evidence of ability to think more critically in other classes in school, at home, in connection with personal problems, and in connection with speeches, advertisements, and arguments. The aspect of critical thinking which appears most susceptible to general improvement is the attitude of being disposed to consider in a thoughtful way the problems and subjects that come within the range of one's experience. An attitude of wanting evidence for beliefs is most subject to general transfer. Development of skill in applying the methods of logical inquiry and reasoning, however, appears to be specifically related to, and in fact limited by, the acquisition of pertinent knowledge and facts concerning the problem or subject matter toward which the thinking is to be directed. There is no reason to believe, for instance, that the students who gained significantly in critical thinking as measured by the tests are now appreciably more competent to make critical judgments of pieces of art, music, or literature.

3. The component abilities involved in critical thinking and measured by the tests developed in connection with this study were found to correlate positively with one another. The

abilities measured by the tests nevertheless are different from one another, as evidenced by low intercorrelations, ranging from .01 to .47, and appear to develop at varying rates, and to be different in their susceptibility to improvement after a short period, such as ten weeks, of instruction.

4. General intelligence, as measured by tests of the type of the Otis Quick-Scoring Mental Ability Test, is something different from the abilities measured by the Watson-Glaser Tests of Critical Thinking, although the intelligence and critical thinking tests overlap and measure common abilities as well as different abilities. The correlation between composite Z-score on the critical thinking tests and the Otis intelligence test was found to be .46.

5. Among the factors measured in this study, intelligence, reading ability, and school marks are most closely related to scores made on the tests of critical thinking. Age, sex, home background rating, and scores on the Interest-Values Inventory were not found to distinguish the top 27 per cent who scored highest from the bottom 27 per cent who scored lowest on the initial administration of the critical thinking tests.

6. Age, sex, average previous school marks, home background rating, and scores on the Interest-Values Inventory were not found to distinguish the top 27 per cent in the experimental group, who gained the most after instruction, from the bottom 27 per cent in the experimental group who gained the least after instruction.

7. Whether a pupil is reactionary or progressive (as these words are defined in A Survey of Opinions Test of the Watson-Glaser tests) in his socio-economic views is not significantly related to whether or not he profits from the kind of training in critical thinking suggested in the lesson units.

8. While there is a tendency for the more intelligent members of a group (as measured by the Otis intelligence test) to profit most from the suggested training in critical thinking, this is only a group trend. Individuals with I. Q.'s of less than 100 are found among those who profit the most from the training. In this study 23 per cent of the thirty-five

students who gained the most among those in the experimental group had I. Q.'s of less than 100. The correlation between gain in (composite Z-score) critical thinking test score and I. Q. for the experimental group was found to be .33.

9. There is a tendency for those who score below the mean of the group on the Watson-Glaser Tests of Critical Thinking before training to show the most gain on these tests after training.

10. The ability to comprehend language with accuracy and discrimination is one of the most important aspects of ability to think critically.

11. The content and suggested procedures described in the lesson units are enjoyable, stimulating, and instructive to many pupils, and are likely to be stimulating for teachers as well.

12. Ratings by four teachers of the experimental classes of eight kinds of pupil behavior regarded as manifestations of ability to think critically were found to correlate .52, .48, .33, and .40 with scores on the critical thinking tests.

13. There is a similarity between the abilities measured by the Watson-Glaser Tests of Critical Thinking and the Martin Reading Comprehension Tests, which is a test of "critical reading." A correlation coefficient of .77 was found between scores on the two tests made by a group of fifty twelfth grade students.

14. The growth in ability to think critically appears to be retained in terms of both retest scores and observable behavior for at least six months after conclusion of the special instruction, and some aspects of the growth which the students experienced probably will be retained more or less permanently and will in turn afford a basis for further growth in ability to think critically.

INTERPRETATION AND CRITIQUE

The critical thinking tests used in connection with this study were much less refined than the revised tests. The data obtained by means of them are not as precise as could be desired. Fortunately, however, the evaluation of the effectiveness of the teaching materials is not limited to the tests. The evaluation by pupils and teachers is in many ways more meaningful and presents more vital evidence of growth toward some of the desired objectives than evaluation by the tests. Quantitative evaluation is a useful and important check upon vague theorizing about the attainment of given outcomes of given educational procedures, but it may leave out a great deal that is significant for understanding the changes in behavior that have taken place.

According to the teacher of experimental class E2:

> The objective testing instruments . . . did not measure my enjoyment in teaching the classes; they did not measure the school-wide interest in the experiment; they did not measure the numerous extemporaneous forays into critical thinking outside of class; they did not measure the requests for admittance to another such course, if it were given; they did not measure the closeness of the associations and the degree of confidence between student and teacher that the give and take informality of class procedure seemed to establish. These are the gains that won't come out in graphs, and yet to me they are as important as an advance of five points in the ability to detect logical fallacies.

The main emphasis in this study was upon the development of teaching procedures and illustration of learning situations which might be immediately useful to the classroom teacher as an aid in realizing one of the cardinal objectives of education—the development of critical thinking. In following this main emphasis, a sacrifice was made of the opportunity to do an intensive study of pupils' patterns of reasoning—of the how, why, and by what means pupils arrive at conclusions about hypothetical, and significant current problems. Only an inadequate beginning in this direction was attempted in the interviews.

All the teachers of the experimental classes felt at the conclusion of the experiment that they could have done a much better job with the units after their first "practice" attempt. They also suggested certain changes in the organization, content, and emphases in the lesson units. These suggestions have been incorporated in the revised units and in the separate textbook now in preparation. Because the tests, the lesson units, and even the teachers involved in this study were not as "good" as they are now, the data obtained from the tests are not as refined as they could be if the experiment were to be repeated under optimum conditions. If the test data were highly precise and refined, the author thinks (on the basis of relationships in the present data) that proper statistical treatment would reveal some valuable data concerning the psychological processes of the pupils participating in the learning situation. It would be especially interesting to ascertain, for example, the correlation between reading scores and critical thinking scores before and after special training in critical thinking, to determine whether the special training results in improved reading ability, and whether certain aspects of the training are useful for "remedial reading."

Such factors as time devoted to teaching for these objectives, the kind and amount of material which is presented, the extent to which self-activity is induced, the amount of meaningful and significant problem-solving in which the students engage, and the ability of the teacher, very likely contribute significantly to the outcomes of instruction. The experiment provides little knowledge about the optimum conditions, or whether there are optimum conditions in a general sense, for the most effective operation of these factors.

PROBLEMS FOR FURTHER STUDY

This study might in some respects be considered a "sharp skirmish" with the problem of the development of critical thinking. Among the problems related to the development of critical thinking which appear especially worth investigating are:

1. What are the most common reasons for errors in the reasoning of children at various levels of mental maturity? By what processes do pupils arrive at the opinions they hold? There are many routes to error in thinking. Which ones are most common at various levels, and how might they best be corrected?

2. What methods other than those suggested in the lesson units can be used with equal or better effect with pupils at different grade levels? What methods are most effective in the least time, and which among the many suggested in the lesson units are most productive for given purposes?

3. To what extent can ability to think critically be improved by adequate remedial reading procedures?

4. What simplification of the materials in the lesson units or what new materials would be suitable for the various levels of the elementary schools and for "slow" groups in the secondary schools?

5. Can "ability to behave intelligently" be improved by training in critical thinking, and can ability to see the relationships required by intelligence tests be improved by a longer period of training than was here attempted?

6. What differences (if any) in actual behavior in emotionally charged situations are manifested by those who have had instruction in critical thinking as compared with equated pupils who have not had such instruction? How do students who have had and who have not had instruction differ in the way they go about attempting to find solutions to community problems to which their attention is directed?

Bibliography

Note: Specific classroom procedures found useful for developing skill in applying the principles of logical reasoning to the solution of problems which are of significance to students are described in those references marked with an asterisk.

1. Abel, T. M. "Unsynthetic Modes of Thinking among Adults: A Discussion of Piaget's Concepts." *American Journal of Psychology,* Vol. 44, pp. 123–132, 1932.

2. *Adler, Mortimer. *How to Read a Book.* Simon and Schuster, New York, 1940.

3. Albig, W. *Public Opinion.* McGraw-Hill Book Company, New York, 1939.

4. Alpert, A. *The Solving of Problem Situations by Pre-School Children: An Analysis.* Contributions to Education, No. 323. Bureau of Publications, Teachers College, Columbia University, 1928.

5. American Institute of Public Opinion. *The New Science of Public Opinion Measurement.* New York, 1939.

6. Annis, A. D. and Meier, N. C. "Induction of Opinion through Suggestion by Means of 'Planted Content.'" *Journal of Social Psychology,* Vol. 5, pp. 65–81, 1934.

7. Arons, L. "Serial Learning and Generalizing Abstraction." *American Journal of Psychology,* Vol. 45, pp. 417–432, 1933.

8. *Ayres, S. "How False Propaganda May Start." *Talks* (Columbia Broadcasting System, New York), Vol. 3, pp. 1–7, 1938.

9. Bain, A. *Education as a Science.* D. Appleton and Company, New York, 1887.

10. Bain, A. *Logic.* Longmans, Green & Co., London, 1892.

11. Bain, A. *The Senses and the Intellect.* John W. Parker and Son, London, 1855.

12. *Baker, G. and Huntington, H. B. *Principles of Argumentation.* Ginn and Company, New York, 1905.

13. Barham, T. C. "A Social Studies Unit that Developed Pupils' Powers of Problem Solving." *Clearing House,* Vol. 12, No. 1, pp. 33–36, 1937.

14. Barlow, M. C. "Transfer of Training in Reasoning." *Journal of Educational Psychology,* Vol. 38, Part 2, pp. 122–128, 1938.

14a. Bartlett, F. C. *Remembering.* The Macmillan Company, New York, 1932.

15. Bateman, R. M. and Remmers, H. H. "The Relationship of Pupil

Attitudes toward Social Topics before and after Studying the Subjects." *Bulletin of Public Opinion,* Vol. 37, pp. 27–42, 1936.

16. Beauchamp, W. D. *Instruction in Science.* United States Office of Education, Bulletin No. 17, Washington, D. C., 1932.

17. Bedell, R. C. "The Relationship between the Ability to Recall and the Ability to Infer in Specific Learning Situations." *Bulletin,* Northeastern Missouri State Teachers College, Vol. 34, No. 9, p. 55, 1934.

18. Bell, E. T. *The Search for Truth.* Reynal and Hitchcock, New York, 1934.

19. Bernays, E. L. *Propaganda.* Horace Liveright and Company, New York, 1928.

20. Biddle, W. W. "Propaganda and the Curriculum." *Curriculum Journal,* Vol. 9, No. 7, pp. 306–308, 1938.

21. Biddle, W. W. *Propaganda and Education.* Bureau of Publications, Teachers College, Columbia University, 1932.

22. Biddle, W. W. "Teaching Resistance to Propaganda." *Seventh Yearbook, National Council for the Social Studies,* 1937.

23. Billings, M. L. "Problem Solving in Different Fields of Endeavor." *The American Journal of Psychology,* Vol. 46, No. 2, pp. 259–272, 1934.

24. Binet, A. *Psychology of Reasoning.* Open Court Publishing Company, Chicago, 1899.

25. Boaz, F. *The Mind of Primitive Man.* Revised Edition. The Macmillan Company, New York, 1938.

26. Bogardus, E. S. "A Social Distance Scale." *Sociology and Social Research,* Vol. 17, pp. 265–271, 1933.

27. Boldt, W. F. and Stroud, J. B. "Changes in the Attitudes of College Students." *Journal of Educational Psychology,* Vol. 25, No. 8, pp. 611–619, 1934.

28. Bolton, E. D. "Effect of Knowledge upon Attitudes toward the Negro." *Journal of Social Psychology,* Vol. 6, pp. 68–90, 1933.

29. Bolton, E. D. "Measuring Specific Attitudes toward the Social Rights of the Negro." *Journal of Abnormal and Social Psychology,* Vol. 31, No. 4, pp. 384–397, 1937.

30. Bonney, M. E. *Techniques of Appeal and Social Control.* George Banta Publishing Co., Menasha, Wis., 1934.

31. Boraas, J. *Teaching to Think.* The Macmillan Company, New York, 1922.

32. Bridges, J. W. "An Experimental Study of Decision Types." *Psychological Review Monograph,* No. 72, 1914.

33. Bridges, J. W. *Psychology, Normal and Abnormal.* D. Appleton-Century Company, New York, 1936.

34. Briggs, T. H. "What the Emotions Do to Our Thinking." *Teachers College Record,* Vol. 36, No. 5, pp. 372–379, 1935.

35. Brigham, C. C. *A Study of Error.* New York College Entrance Examination Board, New York, 1932.

36. Broome, E. C. "Report of the Committee on Propaganda-Abstract." *National Education Association Proceeding and Addresses,* Vol. 67, pp. 204–217, 1929.

37. Budkiewicz, J. "Contributions to the Psychology of Defective Learning." *Kwart. Psychol.* Vol. 7, pp. 81–138, 1935.

38. Brown, Rollo. *How the French Boy Learns to Write.* Harvard University Press, 1915.

39. Bunch, M. E. "The Amount of Transfer in Rational Learning as a Function of Time." *Journal of Comparative Psychology,* Vol. 22, No. 3, pp. 325, 337, 1936.

39a. Buros, Oscar K. (Editor). *The Nineteeen Forty Mental Measurements Yearbook.* The Mental Measurements Yearbook, Highland Park, N. J., 1941.

40. Burt, C. "The Development of Reasoning in School Children." *Journal of Experimental Pedagogy,* Vol. 5, pp. 67–77, 121–127, 1920.

41. Burt, C. *Mental and Scholastic Tests.* P. S. King and Son, Ltd., London, 1933.

42. Burtt, E. A. *Principles and Problems of Right Thinking.* Harper and Brothers, New York, 1931.

43. Caldwell, O. A. "Summary of Investigations Regarding Superstitions and Other Unfounded Beliefs." *Science Education,* Vol. 20, No. 1, pp. 1–4, 1936.

44. Caldwell, O. and Lundeen, C. E. "Changing Unfounded Beliefs—A Unit in Biology." *School Science and Mathematics,* Vol. 33, pp. 394–413, 1933.

45. Campbell, H. "Prejudiced Thinking of School Children." *Teachers Journal and Abstract,* Vol. 5, No. 6, pp. 443–448, 1930.

46. Canby, H. S. "Propaganda That Is Good." *Saturday Review of Literature,* Vol. 13, No. 22, p. 8, March 28, 1936.

47. Cannon, W. B. *Bodily Changes in Pain, Hunger, Fear and Rage.* D. Appleton-Century Company, New York, 1915.

48. Carmichael, P. D. *The Logic of Discovery.* The Open Court Publishing Company, Chicago, 1930.

49. Carroll, R. P. *An Experimental Study of Comprehension in Reading.* Teachers College, Columbia University, 1926.

50. Carroll, R. P. "Can Reasoning Be Taught?" *Journal of Education,* Vol. 114, No. 16, pp. 17–21, 1931.

51. Caswell, H. L. "The Schools and Social Progress." *School Executives Magazine,* Vol. 51, No. 10, pp. 435–437, 1932.

52. Chant, S. N. F. "An Objective Experiment on Reasoning." *American Journal of Psychology,* Vol. 45, No. 2, pp. 282–291, 1933.

53. Chase, S. *The Tyranny of Words.* Harcourt Brace, New York, 1938.

54. Chen, H. S. *The Comparative Coachability of Certain Types of Intelligence Tests.* Contributions to Education, No. 338. Bureau of Publications, Teachers College, Columbia University, 1928.

55. Chen, H. S. "Sex Differences in Simple Syllogistical Judgment." *Pedagogical Seminary,* Vol. 50, No. 1, pp. 3–13, 1937.

56. Chen, W. K. C. "Retention of the Effect of Oral Propaganda." *Journal of Social Psychology,* Vol. 7, pp. 470–483, 1936.

57. Cherrington, B. M. and Miller, L. W. "Changes in Attitude as the Result of a Lecture and Reading Similar Materials." *Journal of Social Psychology,* Vol. 4, pp. 479–484, 1933.

58. Chou, S. K., Chen, H. P., and Chao, W. H. "Sex Differences in Syllogistic Judgment." *Chung Hwa Educational Review,* Vol. 23, No. 5, pp. 41–47, 1935.

59. Claparède, E. "La Decouverte De L'Hypothese." *Journal de Psychologie,* Vol. 29, pp. 646–656, 1933.

60. Claparède, E. "La Genese de l'Hypothese." *Archive de Psychologie,* Vol. 24, p. 155, 1933.

61. Clark, J. A. "Some Aids to Reflective Thinking." *National Education Association, Addresses and Proceedings,* pp. 432–534. Washington D.C., 1932.

62. Clark, B. "Founding the Curriculum on the Scientific Attitude Method." *Teachers College Journal,* Vol. 4, pp. 145–154, 1932.

63. *Clark, E. L. *The Art of Straight Thinking.* D. Appleton-Century Company, New York, 1939.

64. Cohen, M. R. *Reason and Nature.* Harcourt, Brace and Company, New York, 1931.

65. *Cohen, M. R. and Nagel, E. *An Introduction to Logic and Scientific Method.* Harcourt, Brace and Company, New York, 1934.

66. Columbia Associates in Philosophy. *Introduction to Reflective Thinking.* Houghton Mifflin Company, Boston, 1923.

67. Colvin, S. S. *The Learning Process.* The Macmillan Company, New York, 1915.

68. Commins, W. D. *Principles of Educational Psychology,* Ronald Press Company, New York, 1937.

69. Cox, P. W. "What Does Democracy Mean for Us?" *The Educational Forum,* Vol. 3, No. 3, pp. 257–276, 1939.

70. Craig, G. S. *Science and Elementary Education.* Ginn and Company, Boston, 1937.

70a. Croxton, W. C. "Pupils' Ability to Generalize." *School Science and Mathematics,* Vol. 36, pp. 627–634, June, 1936.

71. Cubberley, E. P. *A Brief History of Education.* Houghton Mifflin Company, Boston, 1922.

72. Curtis, F. D. "A Determination of the Scientific Attitudes." *Journal of Chemical Education,* Vol. 3, pp. 920–927, August, 1926.

73. Curtis, F. D. *Some Values Derived from Extensive Reading of General Science.* Contributions to Education, No. 163. Bureau of Publications, Teachers College, Columbia University, 1934.

74. Curtis, F. D. "Some Contributions of Research to Practices in Science Teaching." *Science Education,* Vol. 19, pp. 117–122, October, 1935.

75. Daily, B. W. *Ability of High School Pupils to Select Essential Data in Solving Problems.* Contributions to Education, No. 190. Bureau of Publications, Teachers College, Columbia University, 1925.

76. *Daily Pantagraph. *Labeling the War News.* The Daily Pantagraph, Bloomington, Ill., 1939.

77. Dale, E. *The News Letter.* Vol. 5, No. 2, Bureau of Educational Research, Ohio State University, 1939.

78. Davis, Ira C. "The Measurement of Scientific Attitudes." *Science Education,* Vol. 19, pp. 117–122, October, 1935.

79. Davis-Dubois, R. "Developing Sympathetic Attitudes Toward Peoples." *Journal of Educational Sociology,* Vol. 9, No. 7, pp. 387–396, 1936.

80. Devnich, G. E. "Words as Gestalten." *Journal of Experimental Psychology,* Vol. 20, pp. 297–300, 1937.

81. Dewey, John. "Education as Politics." *New Republic,* Vol. 32, pp. 139–141, 1922.

82. *Dewey, John. *How We Think.* D. C. Heath and Company, New York, 1933.

83. Dewey, John. *Logic: The Theory of Inquiry.* Henry Holt and Company, New York, 1938.

84. Dimnet, E. *The Art of Thinking.* Simon and Schuster, New York, 1928.

85. Doob, L. W. *Propaganda.* Henry Holt and Company, New York, 1935.

86. Downing, E. R. "Does Science Teach Scientific Thinking?" *Science Education,* Vol. 17, No. 2, pp. 87–89, 1933.

87. Downing, E. R. "The Elements and Safeguards of Scientific Thinking." *The Scientific Monthly,* Vol. 16, No. 3, pp. 241–243, 1938.

88. Downing, E. R. "Some Results of a Test on Scientific Thinking." *Science Education,* Vol. 20, No. 3, pp. 121–128, 1936.

89. Downing, E. R. "Scientific Attitude and Skill in Thinking." *School Science and Mathematics,* Vol. 34, pp. 202–203, 1934.

90. Duncker, K. *Zur Psychologie des produktiven Denkens.* Julius Springer, Berlin, Germany, 1935.

90a. Dunn, M. F. *The Psychology of Reasoning.* Williams & Wilkins, Baltimore, 1926.

91. Eckels, C. F. "Clear Thinking Through Use of Physical Science." *California Journal of Social Education,* Vol. 11, pp. 56–57, 1936.

92. Educational Policies Commission. *Learning the Ways of Democracy.* National Education Association, Washington, D. C., 1940.

93. Educational Policies Commission. *The Purposes of Education in American Democracy.* National Education Association, Washington, D. C., 1938.

94. Edwards, N. *Equal Educational Opportunity for Youth.* American Council on Education, Washington, D. C., 1939.

95. *Edwards, V. *Group Leader's Guide to Propaganda Analysis.* Institute for Propaganda Analysis, New York, 1938.

96. Eidens, H. "Experimentelle Untersuchungen über den Denkverlauf bei unmittelbaren Folgerungen." *Archive für die gesamte Psychologie,* Vol. 71, pp. 1–66, 1929.

97. *Ellis, E. (Editor). "Education Against Propaganda." *Seventh Yearbook, National Council for the Social Studies.* McKinley Publishing Company, Philadelphia, 1937.

98. Ewert, P. H. and Lambert, J. C. "The Effect of Verbal Instructions upon the Formation of a Concept." *Journal of Genetic Psychology,* Vol. 6, Part 2, pp. 400–413, 1932.

99. *Fawcett, H. P. *The Nature of Proof.* Thirteenth Yearbook, The National Council of Teachers of Mathematics. Bureau of Publications, Teachers College, Columbia University, 1938.

100. Fowler, H. L. "The Development of Concepts." *British Journal of Educational Psychology,* Vol. 1, No. 1, pp. 13–40, 1931.

101. *Frederick, R. W. *How to Study Handbook.* D. Appleton-Century Company, New York, 1938.

102. Frutchey, F. P. "Testing for Application of Scientific Method," *Educational Method,* Vol. 15, pp. 427–432, 1936.

103. Fryklund, V. "Problem Solving Attitudes." *Industrial Education Magazine,* Vol. 39, No. 5, pp. 255–258, 1937.

104. *Gans, Roma. *Critical Reading Comprehension in the Intermediate Grades.* Contributions to Education, No. 811, Bureau of Publications, Teachers College, Columbia University, 1940.

105. Garrett, H. E. and Fisher, T. R. "The Prevalence of Certain Popular Misconceptions." *Journal of Applied Psychology,* Vol. 10, No. 4, pp. 411–420, 1926.

106. Gates, A. I. and Van Alstyne, D. "The General and Specific Effects of Training in Reading with Observations on the Experimental Technique." *Teachers College Record,* Vol. 25, pp. 98–123, 1924.

107. Gengerelli, J. A. "Mutual Interference in the Evolution of Concepts." *American Journal of Psychology,* Vol. 38, pp. 639–646, 1927.

108. George, W. *The Scientist in Action.* Emerson Books, New York, 1938.

109. Glaser, E. M. and Maller, J. B. "The Measurement of Interest-Values." *Character and Personality,* Vol. 9, pp. 67–81, 1940.

110. Gibson, E. J. and McGarvey, H. R. "Experimental Studies of Thought and Reasoning." *The Psychological Bulletin,* Vol. 34, No. 6, pp. 327–350, 1937.

111. Gray, W. S. *The Teaching of Reading: A Second Report,* National Society for the Study of Education, Thirty-Sixth Yearbook, Public School Publishing Company, Bloomington, Ill., 1937.

112. Greene, E. B. "Certain Aspects of Lecture, Reading and Guided Reading." *School and Society,* Vol. 39, pp. 619–624, 1934.

113. Grim, P. R. "Interpretation of Data and Reading Ability in the Social Studies." *Educational Research Bulletin,* Vol. 19, pp. 372–374, 1940.

114. *Guiler, W. S. and Coleman, S. H. *Getting the Meaning.* J. B. Lippincott Company, New York, 1940.

115. Haggerty, M. E. "The Paramount Service of Education to Society." *Annals of the American Academy of Political and Social Science,* Vol. 182, pp. 10–20, 1935.

116. Hall, E. Loetzer. "Applying Geometric Methods of Thinking to Life Situations." *The Mathematics Teacher,* Vol. 31, pp. 379–384, 1938.

117. Harris, J. A. "Errors of Judgment." *Psychological Review,* Vol. 22, p. 490, 1915.

118. Harter, G. L. "Overt Trial and Error in the Problem Solving of Pre-school Children." *Journal of Genetic Psychology,* Vol. 28, pp. 361–372, 1930.

119. Hartmann, G. W. "A Field Experiment on the Comparative Effectiveness of 'Emotional' and 'Rational' Political Leaflets in Determining Election Results." *Journal of Abnormal and Social Psychology,* Vol. 31, No. 1, pp. 99–114, 1936.

120. Hartung, M. L. "Some Problems in Evaluation." *Mathematics Teacher,* Vol. 31, pp. 175–182, 1938.

121. Hazlitt, H. *Thinking as a Science.* E. P. Dutton and Company, New York, 1916.

122. Hazlitt, V. "Children's Thinking." *British Journal of Psychology,* Vol. 20, pp. 354–361, 1929–30.

123. Healy, W. and Bronner, A. F. *New Light on Delinquency.* Yale University Press, 1936.

124. Heidbreder, E. "Problem Solving in Children and Adults." *Journal of Genetic Psychology,* Vol. 35, No. 4, pp. 522–545, 1928.

125. Heidbreder, E. "A Study of the Evolution of Concepts." *Psychological Bulletin,* Vol. 31, No. 9, p. 673, 1934.

126. Helseth, E. O. *Children's Thinking.* Contributions to Education, No. 209, Bureau of Publications, Teachers College, Columbia University, 1926.

127. Herrick, J. H. "The Evolution of Certain Aspects of Thinking in the

Social Studies." *Educational Method,* Vol. 15, No. 8, pp. 422–426, 1936.

128. Hill, M. *Training to Reason.* Melbourne University Press, Melbourne, Australia, 1936.

129. Hoff, A. G. *A Test for Scientific Attitude.* University of Iowa Thesis, 1930.

130. Hollingworth, H. L. "The Conditions of Verbal Configuration." *Journal of Experimental Psychology,* Vol. 18, pp. 299–306. 1935.

131. Hollingworth, H. L. *Experimental Studies in Judgment.* Science Press, New York, 1915.

132. *Holmes, R. W. *The Rhyme of Reason.* D. Appleton-Century Company, New York, 1939.

133. Horn, E. *Methods of Instruction in the Social Studies.* Charles Scribner's Sons, New York, 1937.

134. Huang, I. "Children's Explanations of Strange Phenomena." *Psychologische Forschung,* Vol. 14, pp. 63–182, 1930.

135. *Hughes, R. O. "Building Public Opinion in a Community." *Ninth Yearbook, National Council for the Social Studies.* McKinley Publishing Company, Philadelphia, 1930.

136. Hume, D. *An Enquiry Concerning Human Understanding.* The Open Court Publishing Company, Chicago, 1904.

137. Hurd, A. W. "Appreciation Objectives in Science Teaching." *School and Society,* Vol. 37, pp. 124–126, 1933.

138. Huse, H. R. *The Illiteracy of the Literate, A Guide to the Art of Intelligent Reading.* D. Appleton-Century Company, New York, 1933.

139. Institute of Educational Research. *I.E.R. Tests of Generalization and Organization.* Teachers College, Columbia University, New York.

140. Institute of Educational Research. *I.E.R. Tests of Selective and Relational Thinking.* Teachers College, Columbia University, New York.

141. *Institute for Propaganda Analysis. *Propaganda Analysis.* Columbia University Press, Vol. 1, 1937–38, Vol. 2, 1938–39, New York.

142. *Institute for Propaganda Analysis. *The Fine Art of Propaganda.* Harcourt, Brace and Company, New York, 1938.

143. James, W. *Psychology, Briefer Course.* Henry Holt and Company, New York, 1892.

144. Jastrow, J. *Effective Thinking.* Simon and Schuster, New York, 1931.

145. Jenness, A. "The Role of Discussion in Changing Opinion Regarding a Matter of Fact." *Journal of Abnormal and Social Psychology,* Vol. 27, No. 3, pp. 279–296, 1932.

145a. Jensen, Kai. "The Social Studies." *Thirty-eighth Yearbook of the National Society for the Study of Education,* Part I, Chap. 17, pp. 325–360. Public School Publishing Co., Bloomington, Ill., 1939.

146. *Jepson, R. W. *How to Think Clearly.* Longmans, Green and Company, New York, 1936.

147. Jewett, A. "Detecting and Analyzing Propaganda." *English Journal,* pp. 105–115, February, 1940.

148. Jones, V. "Attitudes of College Students and the Changes in Such Attitudes During Four Years in College." *Journal of Educational Psychology,* Vol. 29, No. 1, pp. 14–25, 114–134, 1938.

149. Judd, C. H. *Education as the Cultivation of the Higher Mental Processes.* The Macmillan Company, New York, 1936.

150. Kelly, T. L. "A Constructive Ability Test." *Journal of Educational Psychology,* Vol. 7, p. 1, 1916.

151. *Kerfoot, J. B. *How to Read.* Houghton Mifflin Company, Boston, 1916.

152. Keyser, C. J. *Thinking about Thinking.* E. P. Dutton & Company, New York, 1926.

153. Kimmel, W. G. "The Unit on Public Opinion in Senior High School Social Studies." *Seventh Year Book, National Council for the Social Studies,* pp. 151–152. McKinley Publishing Company, Philadelphia, 1937.

154. King, I. *Education for Social Efficiency.* D. Appleton-Century Company, New York, 1913.

155. Kirby, B. C. "Teaching to Think." *Journal of Education,* Vol. 116, No. 14, pp. 363–364, 1933.

156. Kitson, H. D. *How to Use Your Mind,* J. B. Lippincott Company, New York, 1926.

157. Knower, F. H. "Experimental Studies of Changes in Attitudes: I. A Study of the Effect of Oral Argument on Changes of Attitudes." *Journal of Social Psychology,* Vol. 6, pp. 315–347, 1935.

158. Köhler, W. *The Mentality of Apes.* Harcourt, Brace and Company, New York, 1925.

159. Kolninger, R. C. "The Attitude Consistency of High School Seniors." *The Education Digest,* Vol. 2, No. 3, pp. 9–11, 1936.

160. Korzybski, A. *Science and Sanity.* The International non-Aristotelian Library Publishing Company, New York, 1933.

161. Kroeger, G. and Dallenbach, K. "Learning and the Relation of Opposition." *American Journal of Psychology,* Vol. 41, No. 3, pp. 432–441, 1929.

162. Kuo, Z. Y. "Behavioristic Experiment on Inductive Inference." *Journal of Experimental Psychology,* Vol. 6, No. 4, pp. 247–293, 1923.

163. LaPiere, R. R. and Farnsworth, R. *Social Psychology,* McGraw-Hill Book Company, New York, 1936.

164. Lasker, B. "Childhood Prejudices." *Child Study,* Vol. 6, No. 5, pp. 107–109, 1929.

165. Lass, A. H. "Whither the Critical Spirit?" *Journal of Education,* Vol. 117, p. 509, November, 1934.

166. Laycock, S. R. *Adaptability to New Situations.* Warwick and York, Baltimore, 1926.

167. Lazar, N. *The Importance of Certain Concepts and Laws of Logic for the Study and Teaching of Geometry.* George Banta Publishing Company, Menasha, Wis., 1938.

168. Lewis, R. S. "Building Pupils' Defenses through a Unit on Propaganda." *Clearing House,* Vol. 13, No. 1, pp. 22–24, 1938.

169. Lichtenstein, A. *Can Attitudes Be Taught?* Studies in Education, No. 21, Johns Hopkins University, 1934.

170. Lindeman, E. "The Goal of American Education." *Survey Graphic,* Vol. 28, p. 570, October, 1939.

171. Lindquist, E. F. *A First Course in Statistics.* Houghton Mifflin Company, Boston, 1938.

172. Lindquist, E. F. *Statistical Analysis in Educational Research.* Houghton Mifflin Company, Boston, 1940.

173. Locke, J. *The Educational Writings of John Locke.* Edited by J. W. Adamson. Longmans, Green and Co., New York, 1912.

174. Longstreet, R. J. "An Experiment with the Thurstone Attitude Scales." *School Review,* Vol. 43, pp. 202–208, 1935.

175. Lorge, I. "Looking 'Em Over: Dissertation Analysis." *Advanced School Digest,* Vol. 4, No. 2, Teachers College, Columbia University, 1939.

176. Lubin, F. "The Development in Pupils of the Power and Habit of Thinking." *High Points,* Vol. 13, No. 10, pp. 32–36, 1931.

177. Lund, F. H. "The Psychology of Belief." *Journal of Abnormal and Social Psychology,* Vol. 20, pp. 63–81, 174–196, 1925–26.

178. *Lyman, R. L. *The Mind at Work.* Scott, Foresman and Company, Chicago, 1924.

179. McConnell, R. "Attitudes Toward Certain Proposed Social Actions as Affected by Defined Educational Content." *Bulletin of Public Opinion,* Vol. 37, pp. 90–104, 1936.

180. McMurray, D. L. "The Evaluation of Propaganda by the Historical Method." *Seventh Yearbook of the National Council for the Social Studies.* McKinley Publishing Company, Philadelphia, 1937.

181. Maier, N. R. F. "An Aspect of Human Reasoning." *British Journal of Psychology,* Vol. 24, pp. 144–153, 1933.

182. Maier, N. R. F. "Reasoning in Children." *Journal of Comparative Psychology,* Vol. 21, No. 3, pp. 357–366, 1936.

183. Maier, N. R. F. "Reasoning and Learning." *Psychological Review,* Vol. 28, No. 4, pp. 332–346, 1931.

184. Maier, N. R. F. "Reasoning in Humans, Part 1: On Direction." *Journal of Comparative Psychology,* Vol. 10, pp. 115–143, 1930.

185. Maier, N. R. F. "Reasoning in Humans. Part 2: The Solution of a Problem and Its Appearance in Consciousness." *Journal of Comparative Psychology,* Vol. 12, No. 2, pp. 181–194, 1934.

186. Maier, N. R. F. "Reasoning in Rats and Human Beings." *Psychological Review,* Vol. 44, No. 5, pp. 365–378, 1937.

187. Maller, J. B. and Glaser, E. M. *The Interest-Values Inventory.* Bureau of Publications, Teachers College, Columbia University, New York, 1939.

188. Maller, J. B. and Lundeen, G. E. "Sources of Superstitious Belief." *The Journal of Educational Research,* Vol. 26, pp. 321–343, 1933.

189. Mander, A. E. *Clearer Thinking.* Watts and Company, London, 1936.

190. Marshall, J. "Procedures for Developing Desirable Pupil Attitudes." *The National Elementary Principal,* Vol. 15, No. 6, pp. 354–384, 1936.

191. Martin, M. E. *The Construction of a Diagnostic Reading Test for Senior High School Students and College Freshmen.* Bureau of Publications, Teachers College, Columbia University, New York. In press.

192. Mathematical Association of America, National Committee on Mathematical Requirements. *Reorganization of Mathematics in Secondary Schools,* 1923.

193. Matheson, E. "A Study of Problem Solving in Pre-School Children." *Child Development,* Vol. 2, pp. 242–262, 1931.

194. Menefee, S. C. "Stereotyped Phrases and Public Opinion." *American Journal of Sociology,* Vol. 43, No. 4, pp. 614–622, 1938.

195. Miles, C. C. "Sex in Social Psychology." *A Handbook of Social Psychology* (C. Murchison, Editor), pp. 683–797. Clark University Press, Worcester, Mass., 1933.

196. Mill, J. *Analysis of the Phenomena of the Human Mind.* Second Edition. Longmans, Green and Company, London, 1878.

197. Miller, B. E. "Thinking in Education." *School and Community,* Vol. 16, No. 8, pp. 443–447, 1930.

198. Miller, C. R. "Propaganda Analysis in Everyday Life." *The American Teacher,* Vol. 23, No. 3, pp. 8-11, 1938.

199. Miller, E. I. *The Psychology of Thinking.* The Macmillan Company, New York, 1915.

200. Miller, R. M. "Superstitions Among College Students." *Sociology and Social Research,* Vol. 13, No. 4, pp. 361–365, 1929.

200a. Minton, Arthur. "A Method for Teaching Thinking." *English Journal,* Vol. 27, pp. 660–666, 1938.

201. Monroe, W. S. and Carter, R. E. *Use of Different Types of Thought Questions in Secondary Schools, and Their Relative Difficulty for*

Students. College of Education, Bureau of Educational Research, Bulletin No. 14, University of Illinois, 1923.

202. Moore, E. B. "A Study of Scientific Attitudes as Related to Factual Knowledge." *School Review*, Vol. 38, pp. 379–386, 1930.

203. Moore, T. V. *The Reasoning Ability of Children in the First Years of School Life.* The Williams & Wilkins Company, Baltimore, Md., 1929.

204. Morgan, J. E. *Horace Mann, His Ideas and Ideals.* National Home Library Foundation, Washington, D. C., 1936.

205. Muller, H. T. "Mental Traits and Heredity." *Journal of Heredity,* Vol. 16, pp. 435–436, 1935.

206. Murphy, C., Murphy, L., and Newcomb, T. *Experimental Social Psychology.* Revised Edition. Harper and Brothers, New York, 1937.

207. Murphy, G. and Likert, R. *Public Opinion and the Individual.* Harper and Brothers, New York, 1938.

208. *National Education Association, Department of Superintendence, Fourteenth Yearbook. *The Social Studies Curriculum.* Washington, D. C., 1936.

209. *National Council for the Social Studies. Seventh Yearbook. *Education against Propaganda.* McKinley Publishing Company, Philadelphia, 1937.

210. National Education Association, Research Division, "Improving Social Studies Instruction." *Research Bulletin,* Vol. 15, pp. 187–260, November 1937.

211. Nelson, E. "Attitudes Sought by Colleges." *School and Society,* Vol. 46, No. 1188, pp. 444–447, 1937.

212. Nelson, E. "Attitudes: 1. Their Nature and Development." *Journal of General Psychology,* Vol. 1, pp. 367–399, 1939.

213. Nelson, E. "Attitudes: 2. Social Attitudes." *Journal of General Psychology,* Vol. 1, pp. 401–416, 1939.

214. Nelson, E. "Attitudes: 3. Their Measurement." *Journal of General Psychology.* Vol. 1, pp. 417–436, 1939.

215. Nelson, M. J. and Denny, E. C. *The Nelson-Denny Reading Test.* Houghton Mifflin Company, Boston, 1929.

216. Nelson, J. H. *Education for Democracy in Our Time.* McGraw-Hill Book Company, New York, 1939.

217. Noll, V. H. "The Habit of Scientific Thinking." *Teachers College Record,* Vol. 35, No. 1, pp. 1–9, 1933.

218. Noll, V. H. "Measuring Scientific Thinking." *Teachers College Record,* Vol. 35, No. 8, pp. 685–693, 1934.

219. Noll, V. H. "Teaching the Habit of Scientific Thinking." *Teachers College Record,* Vol. 35, No. 3, pp. 202–212, 1933.

220. Ogden, C. K. and Richards, I. A. *The Meaning of Meaning.* Inter-

national Library of Psychology, Philosophy, and Scientific Method. Harcourt, Brace and Company, New York, 1923.

221. Ohio State University, Class of 1934 of the University High School. *Were We Guinea Pigs?* Henry Holt and Company, New York, 1938.

222. Osborne, W. W. "Teaching Resistance to Propaganda." *Journal of Experimental Education,* Vol. 8, pp. 1–17, 1939.

223. Otis, A. S. *Otis Quick-Scoring Mental Ability Tests.* World Book Company, Yonkers, N. Y., 1937.

224. Overstreet, H. A. "Words We Live By." *Parents' Magazine,* Vol. 13, No. 11, p. 15, 1938.

225. Parker, E. "Teaching Pupils the Conscious Use of a Technique of Thinking." *The Mathematics Teacher,* Vol. 17, No. 4, pp. 191–201, 1924.

226. Patterson, C. H. *Principles of Correct Thinking.* Longmans, Green and Company, New York, 1937.

227. Peregrene, D. "The Effect of Printed Social Stimulus Material upon the Attitudes of High School Pupils toward the Negro." *Bulletin of Purdue University,* No. 37, pp. 55–69, 1936.

228. Perrin, P. and Ward, F. *Writing Good English.* Scott, Foresman and Company, Chicago, 1940.

229. Perry, W. M. *A Study in the Psychology of Learning in Geometry.* Contributions to Education, No. 179, Teachers College, Columbia University, New York, 1925.

230. Peterson, G. M. "An Empirical Study of the Ability to Generalize." *Journal of General Psychology,* Vol. 6, pp. 90–114, 1932.

231. Piaget, J., et al. *Judgment and Reasoning in the Child.* Harcourt, Brace and Company, New York, 1928.

232. Piaget, J. *The Language and Thought of the Child.* Harcourt, Brace and Company, New York, 1926.

233. Piaget, J. *Moral Judgment of the Child.* Harcourt, Brace and Company, New York, 1932.

234. Pillsbury, W. B. *The Psychology of Reasoning.* D. Appleton and Company, New York, 1910.

235. Pintner, R. *Intelligence Testing, Methods and Results.* Henry Holt and Company, New York, 1931.

236. Powers, F. F. "The Influences of Intelligence and Personality Traits upon False Beliefs." *Journal of Social Psychology,* Vol. 2, No. 4, pp. 490–493, 1931.

237. Powers, S. R. "The Effects of Instruction in Science on Thought, Feeling, and Action." *Teachers College Record,* Vol. 41, No. 5, p. 405, 1940.

238. Prescott, D. A. *Emotion and the Educative Process.* American Council on Education, Washington, D. C., 1938.

239. Proceedings of the Congress on Education for Democracy. *Education for Democracy.* Bureau of Publications, Teachers College, Columbia University, New York, 1939.

240. *Progressive Education Association. *Evaluation in the Eight Year Study,* Set of Tests Developed in Connection with the Evaluation Program. University of Chicago, 1939.

241. Progressive Education Association, Committee on Secondary School Curriculum. *Language in General Education.* D. Appleton-Century Company, New York, 1940.

242. Progressive Education Association, Committee on Secondary School Curriculum. *Science in General Education.* D. Appleton-Century Company, New York, 1938.

243. Rand, H. "To Teach Thinking." *English Journal* (College Edition), Vol. 24, No. 5, pp. 375–381, 1935.

244. Rees, H. and Israel, H. "An Investigation of the Establishment and Operation of Mental Sets." *Psychological Monographs,* Vol. 46, No. 6, pp. 1–26, 1935.

245. Remmers, H. H. "Propaganda in the Schools—Do the Effects Last?" *Public Opinion Quarterly,* Vol. 2, No. 2, pp. 197–211, 1938.

246. Remmers, H. H. "An Experiment in the Retention of Attitudes as Changed by Instructional Materials." *Studies in Higher Education.* Purdue University, Vol. 34, pp. 20–22, 1938.

247. Richards, I. A. *Interpretation in Teaching.* Harcourt, Brace and Company, New York, 1938.

248. Richards, I. A. *The Philosophy of Rhetoric.* Oxford University Press, New York, 1936.

249. Richards, I. A. *Practical Criticism.* Harcourt, Brace and Company, New York, 1929.

250. Rignano, E. *The Psychology of Reasoning.* Harcourt, Brace and Company, New York, 1923.

251. Roberts, H. D. "Straight Thinking Versus Crooked." *National Parent-Teacher Magazine,* Vol. 33, pp. 30–33, 1939.

252. Roberts, K. E. "The Ability of Pre-School Children to Solve Problems in Which a Simple Principle of Relationship Is Kept Constant." *Journal of Genetic Psychology,* Vol. 40, pp. 118–133, 1932.

253. Roberts, K. E. "Learning in Pre-School and Orphanage Children." *Iowa University Studies in Child Welfare,* Vol. 7, No. 3, p. 94, 1933.

254. Roslow, S. A. "A Statistical Analysis of Rational Learning Problems." *Journal of Genetic Psychology,* Vol. 48, pp. 441–467, 1936.

255. Ruger, H. A. "The Psychology of Efficiency." *Archives of Psychology,* No. 15, 1910.

256. Salisbury, R. "A Study of the Transfer Effects of Training in Logical Organization." *Journal of Educational Research,* Vol. 28, No. 4, pp. 241–254, December, 1934.

257. *Salisbury, R. *Better Work Habits.* Scott, Foresman and Company, Chicago, 1935.

258. Schmidt, C. A. "Teaching Boys to Think." *Agricultural Education,* Vol. 3, No. 8, pp. 122 ff., 1931.

259. Schuchardt, C. R. "Scientific Thinking Among High School Pupils as Shown by Tests." Unpublished Master's Thesis, Department of Education, University of Chicago, 1932.

260. Schuman, S. "Reflective Thinking—in Practice." *High Points,* Vol. 16, pp. 24–28, 1934.

261. Scott, F. and Myers, G. C. "Children's Empty and Erroneous Concepts of the Commonplace." *Journal of Educational Research,* Vol. 8, pp. 327–334, 1923.

262. Selberg, E. M. and Bernard, J. D. "Teaching Pupils the Method for Solving Problems." *Educational Method,* Vol. 16, No. 8, pp. 413–416, 1937.

263. Sells, S. B. "The Atmosphere Effect: An Experimental Study of Reasoning." *Archives of Psychology,* No. 200, New York, 1936.

264. Sells, S. B. and Koob, H. F. "A Classroom Demonstration of 'Atmosphere Effect' in Reasoning." *Journal of Educational Psychology,* Vol. 28, pp. 514–518, 1937.

265. Selz, O. *Zur Psychologie des Produktiven Denkens und des Irrtums. Eine Experimentelle Untersuchung.* F. Cohen, Bonn, 1922.

266. Shaffer, L. F. *Children's Interpretations of Cartoons.* Bureau of Publications, Teachers College, Columbia University, New York, 1930.

267. Shendarkar, D. D. "An Experimental Investigation in Teaching to Solve Problems in Arithmetic and the Light it Throws on the Doctrine of Formal Training." *Indian Journal of Psychology,* Vol. 6, pp. 27–41, 1931.

268. Siipola, E. M. "A Group Study of Some Effects of Preparatory Set." *Psychological Monograph,* Vol. 46, No. 210, pp. 27–38, 1935.

269. *Simon, H. W. *Preface to Teaching.* Oxford University Press, New York, 1938.

270. Simpson, R. H. *Study of Those Who Influence and of Those Who Are Influenced in Discussion.* Bureau of Publications, Teachers College, Columbia University, New York, 1938.

271. Sinclair, J. H. and Tolman, R. S. "An Attempt to Study the Effect of Scientific Training upon Prejudice and Illogicality of Thought." *Journal of Educational Psychology,* Vol. 35, No. 5, pp. 362–370, 1933.

272. Smith, F. T. *Experiment in Modifying Attitudes toward the Negro.* Bureau of Publications, Teachers College, Columbia University, New York, 1933.

273. Smith, O. *Logical Aspects of Measurements.* Columbia University Press, New York, 1938.

274. Smoke, K. L. "An Objective Study of Concept Formation." *Psychological Monograph,* Vol. 67, No. 4, p. 46, 1932.

275. Sommers, K. "Propaganda, An English Project." *English Journal* (High School Edition), Vol. 27, No. 7, pp. 598–600, 1938.

276. Spaulding, F. T. *High School and Life.* McGraw-Hill Book Company, New York, 1939.

277. Spearman, C. *The Nature of Intelligence and the Principles of Cognition.* The Macmillan Company, New York, 1923, 1927.

278. *Stanford Language Arts Investigation. *An Introduction to Interpretation,* by Schiferl, M. Stanford University Press, Palo Alto, Calif., 1939.

279. *Stebbing, L. S. *Thinking to Some Purpose.* Penguin Books, Ltd., Harmondsworth, Middlesex, England, 1939.

280. Strang, R. M. *Problems in the Improvement of Reading in High School and College.* Science Press Printing Company, Lancaster, Penn., 1938.

281. Strasheim, J. J. *A New Method of Mental Testing.* Warwick and York, Baltimore, 1926.

282. Strauss, S. "Some Results for the Test of Scientific Thinking." *Science Education,* Vol. 16, pp. 89–93, 1931.

283. Strong, E. K. "Control of Propaganda as a Psychological Problem." *Scientific Monthly,* Vol. 14, pp. 234–252, 1922.

284. Strong, E. K. *Psychological Aspects of Business.* McGraw-Hill Book Company, New York, 1938.

285. Studebaker, J. W. "Democracy Moves Forward." *Education for Democracy.* Bureau of Publications, Teachers College, Columbia University, New York, 1939.

286. *Symonds, P. M. *Education and the Psychology of Thinking.* McGraw-Hill Book Company, New York, 1936.

287. Tead, O. *New Adventures in Democracy.* McGraw-Hill Book Company, New York, 1939.

288. Teller, J. D. "Improving Ability to Interpret Educational Data." *Educational Research Bulletin,* Vol. 19, pp. 363–371, 1940.

289. Terman, L. M. *The Measurement of Intelligence.* Houghton Mifflin Company, Boston, 1916.

290. Terman, L. M. and Merrill, M. A. *Measuring Intelligence.* Houghton Mifflin Company, New York, 1937.

291. Thorndike, E. L. "The Effect of Changed Data on Reasoning." *Journal of Experimental Psychology,* Vol. 5, No. 1, pp. 33–38, 1922.

292. Thorndike, E. L. "Mental Discipline in High School Studies." *Journal of Educational Psychology,* Vol. 15, No. 1, pp. 1–22, 1924.

293. Thorndike, E. L. "The Psychology of Thinking in the Case of Reading," *Psychological Review,* Vol. 24, p. 220, 1917.

294. Thorndike, E. L. *The Original Nature of Man.* Vol. I, *Educational*

Psychology. Bureau of Publications, Teachers College, Columbia University, 1926.

295. Thorndike, E. L. "Reading as Reasoning." *Journal of Educational Psychology,* Vol. 8, No. 6, pp. 323–332, 1917.

296. *Thouless, R. H. *How to Think Straight.* Simon and Schuster, New York, 1939.

297. Thurstone, L. L. *Nature of Intelligence.* Harcourt, Brace and Company, New York, 1926.

298. Thwing, C. F. "College Students as Thinkers." *North American Review,* Vol. 18, p. 629, 1906.

299. Timmons, W. M. *Decisions and Attitudes as Outcomes of the Discussion of a Social Problem.* Contributions to Education, No. 777. Bureau of Publications, Teachers College, Columbia University, New York, 1939.

300. Titchener, E. B. *Lectures on the Experimental Psychology of the Thought Processes.* The Macmillan Company, New York, 1909.

301. Traxler, A. E. "Problem of Group Remedial Reading in the Secondary School." *High Points,* Vol. 11, pp. 5–18, 1938.

302. Tyler, R. W. "Appraising Progressive Schools." *Educational Methods,* Vol. 15, pp. 412–415, May, 1936.

303. Tyler, R. W. "Evaluation: A Challenge to Progressive Education." *Educational Research Bulletin,* Ohio State University, Vol. 15, No. 1, 1935.

304. Tyler, R. W. "Measuring the Results of College Instruction," *Educational Research Bulletin,* Ohio State University, Vol. 11, pp. 253–260, 1932.

305. Tyler, R. W. "The Relation between Recall and Higher Mental Processes," Chap. II in Judd, C. H., *Education as Cultivation of the Higher Mental Processes.* The Macmillan Company, New York, 1936.

306. Tyler, R. W. "Techniques in Evaluating Behavior." *Educational Research Bulletin,* Ohio State University, Vol. 8, No. 1, 1934.

307. Uhl, W. L. "Finding Problems While Reading." *Elementary English Review,* Vol. 11, No. 4, pp. 94–96, et seq., 1934.

308. Updegraff, R. and Keister, M. E. *A Study of Children's Reactions to Failure and an Experimental Attempt to Modify Them.* University of Iowa Studies in Child Welfare, Vol. 13, No. 4, 1937.

309. University of Michigan, Bureau of Educational Reference and Research. *The Evaluation of Instruction,* 1939.

310. Van Duzer, C. H. "The Meaning of Propaganda." *Social Frontier,* Vol. 4, No. 35, May, 1938.

311. Virginia State Board of Education. *Tentative Course of Study for the Elementary Schools,* Vol. 70, Bulletin No. 5, 1939.

312. Washburn, M. F. "Mathematical Ability, Reasoning and Academic

Standing." *The American Journal of Psychology,* Vol. 50, pp. 484–488, 1937.

313. Waters, R. H. "The Influence of Tuition upon Ideational Learning," *Journal of General Psychology,* Vol. 1, pp. 534–549, 1928.

314. Watson, G. B. *The Measurement of Fair-mindedness.* Contributions to Education, No. 176, Bureau of Publications, Teachers College, Columbia University, New York, 1925.

315. *Watson, G. B. and Glaser, E. M. *The Watson-Glaser Tests of Critical Thinking.* World Book Company, Yonkers-on-Hudson, New York. In press.

316. Wegrocki, H. J. "The Effect of Prestige Suggestibility on Emotional Attitudes." *Journal of Social Psychology,* Vol. 5, No. 3, pp. 384–394, 1934.

317. Wellman, B. L. "Sex Differences." *A Handbook of Child Psychology* (C. Murchinson, Editor), pp. 626–649. Clark University Press, Worcester, Mass., 1933.

318. Wheeler, R. H. "The Development of Meaning." *American Journal of Psychology,* Vol. 33, pp. 223–233, 1922.

319. White, E. E. "A Study of the Possibility of Improving Habits of Thought in School Children by a Training in Logic." *British Journal of Educational Psychology,* Vol. 6, Part 3, pp. 267–273, 1936.

320. Whittaker, M. L. "The Measurement of Attitudes Toward Current Political and Economic Problems Among Junior and Senior High School Pupils." *Journal of Experimental Education,* Vol. 2, No. 1, pp. 64–92, 1933.

321. Wilcocks, R. W. "On Substitution as a Cause of Errors in Thinking." *American Journal of Psychology,* Vol. 40, pp. 26–50, 1928.

322. Wilhelm, W. "Beiträge zur Psychologie des Schliessens." *Archive für die gesamte Psychologie,* Vol. 89, pp. 371–428, 1933.

323. Wilke, W. H. "An Experimental Comparison of the Speech, the Radio, and the Printed Page as Propaganda Devices." *Archives of Psychology,* No. 169, p. 32, 1934.

324. Wilkins, M. C. "The Effect of Changed Material on Ability to Do Formal Syllogistic Reasoning." *Archives of Psychology,* Vol. 16, No. 103, pp. 1–83, 1928.

325. Wilson, H. E. *Education for Citizenship.* McGraw-Hill Book Company, New York, 1938.

326. Winch, W. H. *Children's Perceptions.* Educational Psychological Monographs, Baltimore, 1914.

327. Winch, W. H. "The Transfer of Improvement in Reasoning in School Children." *British Journal of Psychology,* Vol. 13, pp. 370–381, 1923.

328. Witty, P. and Kopel, D. *Reading and the Educative Process.* Ginn and Company, Boston, 1939.

329. Wood, B. D. and Beers, F. S. "Knowledge versus Thinking?" *Teachers College Record*, Vol. 37, pp. 487–499, 1936.

330. Woodworth, R. S. *General Psychology*. Henry Holt and Company, New York, 1931.

331. Wilson, H. E. *Education for Citizenship*. McGraw-Hill Book Company, New York, 1938.

332. Woodworth, R. S. and Sells, S. B. "Atmosphere Effect in Syllogistic Reasoning." *Journal of Experimental Psychology*, Vol. 18, No. 4, pp. 451–460, 1935.

333. Woodworth, R. S. and Thorndike, E. L. "The Influence of Improvement in One Mental Function upon the Efficiency of Other Functions." *Psychological Review*, Vol. 8, No. 3, pp. 247–261, 1901.

334. Wooley, H. T. *An Experimental Study of Children*. The Macmillan Company, New York, 1926.

335. Wrightstone, J. W. *Appraisal of Experimental High School Practices*. Bureau of Publications, Teachers College, Columbia University, New York, 1936.

336. Wrightstone, J. W. *Appraisal of Newer Elementary School Practices*. Bureau of Publications, Teachers College, Columbia University, New York, 1938.

337. Wrightstone, J. W. *A Test of Critical Thinking in the Social Studies*. Bureau of Publications, Teachers College, Columbia University, New York, 1938.

338. Young, D. "Some Effects of a Course in American Race Problems on the Race Prejudice of 450 Undergraduates of the University of Pennsylvania." *Journal of Abnormal and Social Psychology*, Vol. 22, No. 3, pp. 235–242, October–December, 1927.

339. Zapf, R. M. "Superstitions of Junior High School Pupils. Part 2, Effect of Instruction on Superstitious Beliefs." *Journal of Educational Research*, Vol. 31, pp. 481–496, 1938.

340. *Zyve, H. L. *Stanford Scientific Aptitude Test*. Stanford University Press, Palo Alto, Calif., 1929.

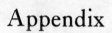

Appendix

TESTS

[Directions and a Sample Question from Each of the
Watson-Glaser Tests of Critical Thinking*]

Test A: A SURVEY OF OPINIONS—SECTION I

Directions: Below are a number of statements which represent opinions about various social problems. Since these statements deal with unsettled questions, *there are no right or wrong answers.* Persons differ in the way they feel about each item. You are to express YOUR point of view about them.

Mark:

(A) U D   If you *agree* with the whole statement.
A (U) D   If you are *undecided* about the opinion expressed.
A U (D)   If you *disagree* with the whole statement.

Work rapidly. Be sure to answer *every* question by placing a circle around one of the three possible answers to the left of the question (A, U, or D).

This is not an examination. There are no *right* answers which you are expected to give. It is merely a request for *your own honest opinion.*

Begin Here:
  1.   A   U   D   In general the wages or salaries persons receive are a fair measure of the value to society of the service they render.

Test A: A SURVEY OF OPINIONS—SECTION II

Directions: (The directions are the same as for Section I).
Begin Here:
  101.   A   U   D   In general, the wages or salaries persons receive are not a fair measure of the value to society of the services they render.

Test B–AR: LOGICAL REASONING TEST
(Area of Abstract Problems)

Directions: (Read Carefully.) Each of the exercises which follow contains two statements (called *premises*) and a conclusion drawn from these premises. The conclusion always begins with the word *Therefore,* and is underlined.
You are to decide whether, *assuming the premises to be true,* the conclusion would *necessarily* have to follow. For example:

(S) U   All cats drink milk.   (Major Premise)
         Susie is a cat.   (Minor Premise)
         Therefore, Susie drinks milk.   (Conclusion)

---

*The tests shown in the Appendix are the preliminary experimental forms; the 1941 revised forms are being printed by the World Book Company, Yonkers-on-Hudson, New York.

The conclusion drawn necessarily follows from the given premises; it is therefore SOUND. Now consider this:

S (U)   All cats drink milk.   (Major Premise)
         Susie drinks milk.   (Minor Premise)
         Therefore, Susie is a cat.   (Conclusion)

This conclusion does not necessarily follow from the given premises; it is therefore UNSOUND. While it is stated that "All cats drink milk," this does not mean that "Only cats, and no other living things, drink milk." Thus, in this case, Susie is not *necessarily* a cat; Susie might be the name of a girl who drinks milk.

Although the premises as stated may or may not be true, for the purposes of this test you are asked to assume that they are true, and to judge whether the conclusions drawn from the premises are SOUND or UNSOUND. As a further example consider the exercise which follows:

(S) U   No musicians are Italians.   (Major Premise)
         All barbers are musicians.   (Minor Premise)
         Therefore, no barbers are Italians. (Conclusion)

Even though the premises themselves really are false, the conclusion above is logically drawn and necessarily follows from the premises as given.

Look at the exercises below. Preceding the number designating each exercise you will find the letters S and U, which stand for the words SOUND and UNSOUND.

SOUND means that the conclusion necessarily follows from the given premises, and is correctly drawn.

UNSOUND means that the conclusion does not necessarily follow from the given premises, and therefore is not correctly drawn.

If you think the conclusion does follow logically, put a circle around the letter S.

If you think the conclusion does not follow logically, put a circle around the letter U.

Judge every conclusion with care. Do not skip any. Work as rapidly as you can without making mistakes.

Begin Here:

S U   1.   Fish live in water.
             Dogs are not fish.
             Therefore, dogs do not live in water.

Test B–SP: LOGICAL REASONING TEST*
(Area of Social Problems)

Directions: (The directions are similar to those for Test B–AR, but with different examples, which pertain to socio-economic-political subjects.)

S U   1.   Self-respecting persons want to work.
             Those on relief are not self-respecting persons.
             Therefore, those on relief do not want to work.

* Test B–SP was not available for use in the experimental study reported in this volume.

Test C: INFERENCE TEST

Directions: Mere facts may mean different things to different people. It is often important to know just what people think certain facts mean. In this test you will find a series of *statements of facts;* and after each statement conclusions which some people would draw from these facts. You are to accept the first statement, the facts, as *true* regardless of whether or not you personally believe them to be so. *You are to be concerned merely with the question of the degree of truth or falsity of the conclusions which have been drawn from the facts.* It is an error in thinking to jump at conclusions without evidence, but it is also an error to be overcautious and to fail to recognize a conclusion as probable or improbable on the basis of the given facts.

At the left of each conclusion you will find the letters T, PT, ID, PF, and F. The meaning of these letters is as follows:

T	means that you think the conclusion is definitely a *true* one; that it properly follows from the statement of fact given in the exercise.
PT	means that you think the conclusion is *probably true;* that the facts in the statement point to the probability of the statement's being true, but that one cannot be entirely sure that it is true on the basis of the facts given in the statement.
ID	means that there are *insufficient data;* that you cannot tell from the facts given whether the conclusion is likely to be true or false.
PF	means that, in the light of the facts given in the statement, you think the conclusion is *probably false;* that the chances are that it is false, but one cannot be entirely sure that it is false.
F	means that you think the conclusion is definitely a *false* one; that it cannot possibly be drawn or inferred from the statement of fact as given in the exercise.

Put a circle around either T, PT, ID, PF, or F at the left of each *conclusion*.

EXAMPLE: *Statement:* Five thousand students recently attended a conference at which questions of race relations and of possible attitudes toward war were discussed, these being the problems the students felt to be most vital today.

Conclusions:

T (PT) ID PF F   (a) The students as a group were of higher than average intelligence.

T PT ID (PF) F   (b) The students were all between the ages of ten and twelve.

T PT (ID) PF F   (c) The students came from all sections of the country.

T PT ID PF (F)   (d) The students came to discuss trade-union problems.

(T) PT ID PF F   (e) The question of attitudes toward war is considered by many students to be important enough to be discussed.

In the above example, conclusion (a) is *probably true* (PT) because of the students' serious concern with important social problems; this implies higher than average intelligence. Conclusion (b) is *probably false* (PF) because children between ten and twelve years of age are not usually so interested in social problems that 5,000 of them would attend such a conference. There is no just evidence for conclusion (c); there are *insufficient data* (ID) for making a judgment in the matter. Conclusion (d) is definitely false (F) because it contradicts the given statement of fact. Conclusion (e) is the only one among those offered which necessarily follows from the given facts; it is therefore *true* (T).

In the exercises which follow, more than one of the conclusions from a given statement may be True, False, Probably True, or Probably False, or have Insufficient Data to warrant a judgment. That is, you are not to assume that there may be only one T, one PT, one ID, one PF, and one F conclusion in connection with each statement as in the example above.

1. *Statement:* Yesterday, a freight elevator in the Main Building fell four stories and struck the bumpers at the bottom of the shaft. The elevator, operated by Michael Jackson, had stopped at the fourth floor to let off part of the cleaning crew. Just as Jackson was about to open the door, the elevator began to drop. Jackson immediately applied the emergency brake, but it did not hold.

Conclusions:

T PT ID PF F (a) The original cause of the accident was a deficient emergency brake.

T PT ID PF F (b) The emergency brake was deficient.

T PT ID PF F (c) The elevator operator tried to stop the elevator from falling.

T PT ID PF F (d) Some of the cleaning crew were very much frightened by the drop.

T PT ID PF F (e) The cleaning crew of the Main Building never uses the passenger elevators in that building.

Test D: GENERALIZATION TEST

Directions: In the two parts of this test you will find some statements which you commonly hear people make, but the first word of each statement has been omitted. Preceding each statement there are five responses—All, Most, Don't Know (DK), Few, No—any one of which might fit in the blank. DRAW A CIRCLE around the one response which you are sure would most truly and accurately complete the sentence. For example:

All Most (DK) Few No—days next year will be rainy days.

All means 100%; without exception. For example, "ALL men are mortal." Most means more than 50%, but less than 100%; more than half. For example, "MOST automobiles use gasoline for fuel." (Some do not; they are run by electricity or by steam.)

Don't Know (how many) means that you do not know whether the statement applies to more or less than 50% of the group in question. For example, "DON'T KNOW (how many) persons are superstitious." We know that there are a considerable number of persons who are superstitious, and we may suspect that they constitute more or less than 50% of the population, but we do not know.

Few means a relatively small number; definitely less than 50%. For example, "FEW people commit suicide."

No means not one; 0%. For example, "NO living person is 500 years old."

Be sure that you do not omit any statements.

Begin Here:

1. All Most DK Few No—people in Boston like to read detective stories.

Test E: DISCRIMINATION OF ARGUMENTS TEST

Directions: In deciding important questions it is necessary to distinguish between strong, important and weak, unimportant ones.

The following exercises consist of a series of questions. Under each question are four statements or arguments which might be put forth in support of either side of the question. Some of these arguments, if regarded as true, would be strong and important arguments in support of or in opposition to the question at issue. Others, even though regarded as true, would nevertheless be weak and relatively unimportant. Read each argument carefully, and *for purposes of this test regard the argument as true;* then decide whether you would call it strong or weak.

If you think it is a strong, important argument applicable to the question and well worth considering, draw a circle around the word STRONG. Wherever you feel the argument is weak and unimportant or not applicable to the question, draw a circle around the word WEAK. *It makes no difference whether the argument is on the side of the question with which you agree or not.* Consider only whether it is a strong or a weak argument, regardless of whether you personally agree with it.

EXAMPLE: Is it desirable for all young men to go to college?

Strong (Weak) If they go to college they will learn the school yells.
Strong (Weak) Some college men are conceited.
(Strong) Weak College is likely to increase their earning powers and culturally enrich their lives.
(Strong) Weak Many young men cannot profit from college work and might better spend those years in more definite vocational training.

It is clear that the first argument advanced above is a rather unimportant and silly reason for spending four years at college. It is therefore marked WEAK. The second reason is also marked WEAK because the statement does not say that all college men are conceited, or that some non-college men are not also conceited. The reason as stated is therefore practically meaningless as an argument against going to college. The last two arguments, however, if taken to be true, would be relatively STRONG, although on opposite sides of the question.

I. Should refugees from religious and political persecution in other countries be granted admission to the United States?

Strong Weak   1. We have not provided jobs for millions of our own citizens at present, and until we solve that problem these refugees would add to the burden of unemployed.

Strong Weak   2. If the United States took some of the refugees, it would help the cause of democracy, freedom, and tolerance at a time when these achievements of civilization are being sorely attacked in many parts of the world.

Strong Weak   3. The United States has always been a haven or refuge for the oppressed from all lands.

Strong Weak   4. Many of the refugees did not obey all the laws in the countries from which they escaped.

Test F 2: EVALUATION OF ARGUMENTS TEST*

Directions: This test contains a number of exercises. Each exercise describes some situation or argument from which a conclusion is drawn. For example:

> In the course of a letter to a newspaper the president of a power and light company said: "The Federal government is building electric power lines which will compete with private power utilities in the Tennessee Valley. It is unfair for the Federal government to compete with private power utilities."

> Assuming these statements to be true, check (√) any of the following conclusions which in your opinion are consistent with them, and can logically be drawn:

.√. 1. It is unfair for the Federal government to build competing power lines in the Tennessee Valley.

.... 2. It is quite fair for the Federal government to build competing power lines in the Tennessee Valley.

.... 3. Further information is needed before any logical conclusion can be drawn.

> Check below (√) any statements which you would use to explain or support your conclusion.

.... a. The power companies have a lot of money invested and the government will ruin their business.

.... b. The word "utilities" needs to be more carefully defined.

.√. c. If a person accepts the original statements, then to be logical he should accept the conclusion which follows from them even if it is not necessarily true.

.... d. We need to know whether the private power companies charge too much.

.... e. The government need not pay taxes to itself so it is unfair for it to compete with private business.

.... f. The people are benefited because competition helps keep the cost of power low.

Since we are told to assume the statement given is true, and since one of the statements given is "It is unfair for the Federal government to compete with private power utilities," and another statement given says that the Federal government *is* building competing lines, then conclusion No. 1 is the one which logically follows, and should therefore be checked. Among the reasons, "c" is the only correct one in support of conclusion No. 1.

In the exercises which follow, you are to check the conclusion which you think can logically be drawn, and in addition, you will be asked to select from a number of statements given, those which you would use to explain your reasoning. Check only those *necessary* to support your conclusions.

READ CAREFULLY THE DIRECTIONS WHICH ACCOMPANY EACH EXERCISE. Do not spend too much time on any one exercise. Answer the easier exercises first, then return to the harder ones. You should be able easily to complete all of them in twenty minutes. If you have any time after you have finished the last exercise, go back and correct any mistakes you may have made. Try to complete all the exercises.

* This test was adapted with permission from a test developed by the Progressive Education Association, Evaluation in the Eight Year Study.

APPENDIX B

STATUS SHEET

[Simply underline your answer to the following questions, except where spaces are provided for written answers.]

Name .... Address ....
Sex .... Age ...... Date of Birth .... Place of Birth ....
Name of School .... Grade ..... Teacher's Name ....
Number of <u>older</u> brothers .... Number of <u>older</u> sisters ....
Number of <u>younger</u> brothers .... Number of <u>younger</u> sisters ....
Reside with parents? Yes No If only one, which ....
Ancestral Descent ....

(1) Father living? Yes No Birthplace .... Occupation ....
(2) Do you have a step-father? Yes No Birthplace ....
    What is your father's (or step-father's) occupation ....
(3) Mother living? Yes No Birthplace .... Occupation ....
(4) Do you have a step-mother? Yes No Birthplace .... Occupation ....
(5) Number of grades father (or step-father) completed in school: (a) 1 to 4, lower elementary grades; (b) 4 to 8, higher elementary grades; (c) 8 to 12, high school; (d) 12 to 16, college; (e) 16 to 19, graduate or professional school.
(6) Number of grades mother (or step-mother) completed in school: (a) 1 to 4, lower elementary grades; (b) 4 to 8, higher elementary grades; (c) 8 to 12, high school; (d) 12 to 16, college; (e) 16 to 19, graduate or professional school.
(7) Are your father and mother living together? Yes No
(8) What is the chief language spoken in your home? (a) ....
    Others (b) ....
(9) How many rooms in your home ....
(10) How many people live in your home? (Count everybody including yourself) ....
(11) Does your family have: (a) A telephone .... (b) A vacuum cleaner .... (c) An electric refrigerator .... (d) a radio .... (e) A piano .... (f) An automobile which is not a truck ....
(12) Did your family go away for a vacation within the past year? ....
(13) Do you have a servant in your home? (a) .... If so, part time (b) .... All the time? (c) ....
(14) Do you have a bank account in your own name? ....
(15) Do you have a public library card? ....
(16) What is your weekly spending money? (Circle the amount that is most nearly correct) None 10¢ 25¢ 50¢ 75¢ $1.00 $2.00 $3.00 $5.00 More
(17) How often do you have your teeth examined? Never .... Once a year .... Oftener ....
(18) Do you play a musical instrument? (a) .... Which ....
    Have you ever taken singing or dancing lessons? (b) ....

(19) Does your family attend concerts? Never .... Occasionally .... Frequently ....
(20) What newspaper (or newspapers) are regularly taken in your home? ....
(21) Do you have your own room in which to study? Yes No
(22) Do you have a hobby? .... If so, what is it? ....
(23) Do you work after school? .... If so, what do you do? ....
(24) What do you usually do in the evening beside homework? ....
(25) Religion ....
(26) Do you attend church (or synagogue) regularly? ....

SCORE KEY

[Guide for Scoring Status Sheet]

CLASSIFICATION OF OCCUPATIONS*

Group I: Professional men, proprietors of large businesses and higher executives, architects, clergymen, mayors, insurance agents who own own business, hotel managers, government and railroad inspectors.

Group II: Commercial service, clerical service, large landowners, managerial service of a lower order than in Group I, and business proprietors employing from five to ten men.
Accountants, large-scale farmers, high-school teachers, insurance agents working for someone else, assistants in governmental employ.

Group III: Artisan proprietors, petty officials, printing trades employees, skilled laborers with some managerial responsibility, business proprietors employing one to five men.
Bakers, barbers, clerks in stores, farmers, foremen, detectives, mail clerks, police sergeants.

Group IV: Skilled laborers (with exception of printers) who work for someone else. Small shop owners doing their own work.
Bakers, carpenters, chefs, janitors, policemen, sailors, waiters.

Group V: Unskilled laborers, venders, unemployed.

Questions 1 through 4 have a maximum score of 10 points and are based only on the *occupation* query: For example, if the father is dead, then the occupation of the step-father should be scored. If no living male member of the family is employed, then the mother's occupation should be scored. If the mother is dead, the step-mother's score for occupation should be used. The scoring is as follows:

Group I — 10 points
Group II — 8 points
Group III— 5 points
Group IV— 2 points
Group V — 0 points.

* This classification relates to questions 1 through 4.

Questions 5 and 6 have a maximum score of 8 points each, as follows:

Professional School   8
College   6
High School   4
Elementary School   2

Question 7: *Yes* = 2 points. *No* = 0.

Question 8: (*a*) English—3 points. (*b*) No credit is given, or taken, for any additional language.

Question 9: The answer for 9 is to be divided by the answer for 10. Score quotient as follows: 0.0 to 0.50 = 0; .51 to 1.00 = 3; 1.01 to 1.50 = 4; 1.51 to 2.00 = 6; 2.01, or more = 8 points.

Question 11: *No* to any of these questions receives 0.
     Yes is scored as follows:
         $a = 4$
         $b = 4$
         $c = 3$
         $d = 2$
         $e = 3$
         $f = 5$. (Maximum score for this question is 21 points.)

Question 12: *Yes* is scored as 4 points. *No* receives 0.

Question 13: If answer to (a) is *yes*, then (b) is scored as 3, or (c) as 6.

Question 14: *Yes* scores 3. *No* is 0.

Question 15: *Yes* scores 2. *No* is 0.

Question 16: Score as follows:
     None equals 0.
     10¢ is 0.
     25¢ is 3.
     50¢ is 4.
     75¢ is 5.
     $1.00, or more scores 6.

Question 17: *Never* scores 0.
     Once scores 3.
     Oftener scores 4.

Question 18: (a) scores 3 if *yes.*
     (b) scores 3 if *yes.*

Question 19: *No* scores 0.
     Occasionally scores 2.
     Frequently scores 5.

Question 20: *Yes*—any one newspaper—scores 3.

Question 21: *Yes* scores 2.

Question 22: *Yes* scores 2.

Questions 23–26 not scored.

PERSONAL DATA

[From the Maller-Glaser Interest-Values Inventory]

Directions: Please answer the following questions by encircling either the word YES or the word NO at the left of each question.

Do you feel that your good qualities are generally appreciated and recognized—

Yes No 1. By your family?

Yes No 2. At work (or at school)?

Yes No 3. Among your friends?

Yes No 4. Do you feel that you are making a success of your job (or your studies)?

Yes No 5. Are you satisfied with your opportunities to advance?

Yes No 6. Are you satisfied with your opportunities to attain your ambitions?

Yes No 7. Are you satisfied with your opportunities to express yourself?

Yes No 8. Do you feel that you are doing (or studying) something really worth while?

Yes No 9. Are you frequently bored? Do you often find life dull and monotonous?

Yes No 10. Does your work tire you out too much?

Yes No 11. Do you have friends of the kind you want, whose company you enjoy and who enjoy your company?

Yes No 12. Do you feel that you have made a satisfactory adjustment in regard to members of the opposite sex?

Yes No 13. Do you often feel just miserable?

Yes No 14. Do you often feel lonesome, even when you are with other people?

Yes No 15. Do you regard yourself as religious?

16. Which gives you more satisfaction: a. Your job (or school)? ....
b. The things you do in your spare time? ....

17. What kinds of recreation give you the most pleasure? ....

18. Describe briefly something that you are now doing (in your work or at school) which gives you a great deal of satisfaction.
....

19. Describe briefly something which at present is causing you dissatisfaction, annoyance, or unpleasantness. (Answers will be held strictly confidential.)
....

20. If you could change something about your school or work which would make you enjoy it more, what would you change? What would you do instead?
....

21. What occupation or vocation do you intend to follow? ....

22. What occupation would you choose if you were able and free to follow any type of work you desired?
....

23. What is your health condition at present? (Check one)
Excellent .... Good .... Fair .... Poor ....

Write your name here .... Sex .... Married? ......

Present occupation .... Age .... Date ....

Grade reached in school .... Major subject in school ....

Which subject do you (or did you) enjoy most? .... Which least? ....